Excel 2003: Advanced

Student Manual

Excel 2003: Advanced

Series Product Managers:	Charles G. Blum and Adam A. Wilcox
Developmental Editor:	Leslie Caico
Keytester:	Michele Jacobson
Series Designer:	Adam A. Wilcox

Trademarks

ILT Series is a trademark of Axzo Press.

Some of the product names and company names used in this book have been used for identification purposes only and may be trademarks or registered trademarks of their respective manufacturers and sellers.

Disclaimers

We reserve the right to revise this publication and make changes from time to time in its content without notice.

*The ProCert Labs numerical rating referenced is based on an independent review of this instructional material and is a separate analysis independent of Certiport or the Microsoft Office Specialist program.

Microsoft, the Office Logo, Excel, Outlook, and PowerPoint are either registered trademarks or trademarks of Microsoft Corporation in the United States and/or other countries. The Microsoft Office Specialist Logo is used under license from owner.

Certiport and the Certiport Approved Courseware logo are registered trademarks of Certiport Inc. in the United States and/or other countries.

Axzo Press is independent from Microsoft Corporation or Certiport, and not affiliated with Microsoft or Certiport in any manner. While this publication may be used in assisting individuals to prepare for a Microsoft Office Specialist exam, Microsoft, Certiport, and Axzo Press do not warrant that use of this publication will ensure passing a Microsoft Office Specialist exam.

ISBNs:

    ISBN-13: 978-1-4188-8937-1 = Student Manual
    ISBN-10: 1-4188-8937-7 = Student Manual
    ISBN-13: 978-1-4188-8939-5 = Student Manual with CDs (student data and CBT)
    ISBN-10: 1-4188-8939-3 = Student Manual with CDs (student data and CBT)

Printed in the United States of America

1 2 3 4 5 GL 09 08 07

What does the Microsoft® Office Specialist Approved Courseware logo represent?

Only the finest courseware receives approval to bear the Microsoft® Office Specialist logo. In order to give candidates the greatest chance of success at becoming a Microsoft Office Specialist, all approved courseware has been reviewed by an independent third party for quality of content and adherence to exam objectives. This specific course has been mapped to the following Microsoft Office Specialist Exam Skill Standards:

- Excel® 2003 Specialist
- Excel 2003 Expert

What is Microsoft Office Specialist certification?

Microsoft Office Specialist certification shows that employees, candidates and students have something exceptional to offer—proven expertise in Microsoft Office programs. Recognized by businesses and schools around the world, it is the only Microsoft-approved certification program of its kind. There are four levels of certification available: Specialist, Expert, Master, and Master Instructor.[1] Certification is available for the following Microsoft Office programs:

- Microsoft Word
- Microsoft Excel
- Microsoft Access
- Microsoft PowerPoint®
- Microsoft Outlook®
- Microsoft Project

For more information

To learn more about becoming a Microsoft Office Specialist, visit www.microsoft.com/officespecialist.

To learn about other Microsoft Office Specialist approved courseware from the ILT Series, visit www.axzopress.com.

---

[1]The availability of Microsoft Office Specialist certification exams varies by Microsoft Office program, program version, and language. Visit www.microsoft.com/officespecialist for exam availability.

Contents

Introduction

After reading this introduction, you will know how to:

A Use ILT Series training manuals in general.

B Use prerequisites, a target student description, course objectives, and a skills inventory to properly set your expectations for the course.

C Re-key this course after class.

Topic A: About the manual

ILT Series philosophy

ILT Series training manuals facilitate your learning by providing structured interaction with the software itself. While we provide text to explain difficult concepts, the hands-on activities are the focus of our courses. By paying close attention as your instructor leads you through these activities, you will learn the skills and concepts effectively.

We believe strongly in the instructor-led classroom. During class, focus on your instructor. Our manuals are designed and written to facilitate your interaction with your instructor, and not to call attention to manuals themselves.

We believe in the basic approach of setting expectations, delivering instruction, and providing summary and review afterwards. For this reason, lessons begin with objectives and end with summaries. We also provide overall course objectives and a course summary to provide both an introduction to and closure on the entire course.

Manual components

The manuals contain these major components:

- Table of contents
- Introduction
- Units
- Appendices
- Course summary
- Quick reference
- Glossary
- Index

Each element is described below.

Table of contents

The table of contents acts as a learning roadmap.

Introduction

The introduction contains information about our training philosophy and our manual components, features, and conventions. It contains target student, prerequisite, objective, and setup information for the specific course.

Units

Units are the largest structural component of the course content. A unit begins with a title page that lists objectives for each major subdivision, or topic, within the unit. Within each topic, conceptual and explanatory information alternates with hands-on activities. Units conclude with a summary comprising one paragraph for each topic, and an independent practice activity that gives you an opportunity to practice the skills you've learned.

The conceptual information takes the form of text paragraphs, exhibits, lists, and tables. The activities are structured in two columns, one telling you what to do, the other providing explanations, descriptions, and graphics.

Appendices

An appendix is similar to a unit in that it contains objectives and conceptual explanations. However, an appendix does not include hands-on activities, a summary, or an independent practice activity. We have also included an appendix that lists all Microsoft Office Specialist exam objectives for Excel 2003 along with references to corresponding coverage in ILT Series courseware.

Course summary

This section provides a text summary of the entire course. It is useful for providing closure at the end of the course. The course summary also indicates the next course in this series, if there is one, and lists additional resources you might find useful as you continue to learn about the software.

Quick reference

The quick reference is an at-a-glance job aid summarizing some of the more common features of the software.

Glossary

The glossary provides definitions for all of the key terms used in this course.

Index

The index at the end of this manual makes it easy for you to find information about a particular software component, feature, or concept.

Manual conventions

We've tried to keep the number of elements and the types of formatting to a minimum in the manuals. This aids in clarity and makes the manuals more classically elegant looking. But there are some conventions and icons you should know about.

Convention	Description
Italic text	In conceptual text, indicates a new term or feature.
Bold text	In unit summaries, indicates a key term or concept. In an independent practice activity, indicates an explicit item that you select, choose, or type.
`Code font`	Indicates code or syntax.
`Longer strings of ▶ code will look ▶ like this.`	In the hands-on activities, any code that's too long to fit on a single line is divided into segments by one or more continuation characters (▶). This code should be entered as a continuous string of text.
Select **bold item**	In the left column of hands-on activities, bold sans-serif text indicates an explicit item that you select, choose, or type.
Keycaps like (↵ ENTER)	Indicate a key on the keyboard you must press.

Hands-on activities

The hands-on activities are the most important parts of our manuals. They are divided into two primary columns. The "Here's how" column gives short instructions to you about what to do. The "Here's why" column provides explanations, graphics, and clarifications. Here's a sample:

Do it!

A-1: Creating a commission formula

Here's how	Here's why
1 Open Sales	This is an oversimplified sales compensation worksheet. It shows sales totals, commissions, and incentives for five sales reps.
2 Observe the contents of cell F4	F4 ▾ = =E4*C_Rate
	The commission rate formulas use the name "C_Rate" instead of a value for the commission rate.

For these activities, we have provided a collection of data files designed to help you learn each skill in a real-world business context. As you work through the activities, you will modify and update these files. Of course, you might make a mistake and, therefore, want to re-key the activity starting from scratch. To make it easy to start over, you will rename each data file at the end of the first activity in which the file is modified. Our convention for renaming files is to add the word "My" to the beginning of the file name. In the above activity, for example, a file called "Sales" is being used for the first time. At the end of this activity, you would save the file as "My sales," thus leaving the "Sales" file unchanged. If you make a mistake, you can start over using the original "Sales" file.

In some activities, however, it may not be practical to rename the data file. If you want to retry one of these activities, ask your instructor for a fresh copy of the original data file.

Topic B: Setting your expectations

Properly setting your expectations is essential to your success. This topic will help you do that by providing:

- Prerequisites for this course
- A description of the target student at whom the course is aimed
- A list of the objectives for the course
- A skills assessment for the course

Course prerequisites

Before taking this course, you should be familiar with personal computers and the use of a keyboard and a mouse. Furthermore, this course assumes that you've completed the following courses or have equivalent experience:

- *Windows 2000: Basic* or *Windows XP: Basic*
- *Excel 2003: Intermediate*

Target student

Before taking this course, you should be comfortable using a personal computer and Microsoft Windows 98 or later. You should have some experience with Excel XP and should be familiar with intermediate-level tasks, such as sorting data, linking worksheets, and showing toolbars. You'll get the most out of this course if your goal is to become proficient in performing advanced tasks, such as creating nested functions, working with data tables, exporting/importing data, performing what-if analyses, recording macros, and publishing worksheets as Web pages.

Microsoft Office Specialist certification

This course is designed to help you pass both Microsoft Office Specialist exams for Excel 2003 (Specialist and Expert). For complete certification training, you should complete this course as well as:

- *Excel 2003: Basic*
- *Excel 2003: Intermediate*

Course objectives

These overall course objectives will give you an idea about what to expect from the course. It is also possible that they will help you see that this course is not the right one for you. If you think you either lack the prerequisite knowledge or already know most of the subject matter to be covered, you should let your instructor know that you think you are misplaced in the class.

Note: In addition to the general objectives listed below, specific Microsoft Office Specialist exam objectives are listed at the beginning of each topic. For a complete mapping of exam objectives to ILT Series content, see Appendix B.

After completing this course, you will know how to:

* Use names to make formulas easier to understand; use the IF and SUMIF functions to calculate a value based on specified criteria; use the nested IF function to evaluate complex conditions; use the ROUND function to round off numbers; and use the PMT function to calculate periodic payments for a loan.

* Use the VLOOKUP function to find a value in a worksheet list; use the MATCH function to find the relative position of a value in a range; use the INDEX function to find the value of a cell at a given position within a range; and use data tables to project values.

* Summarize worksheet data by creating automatic subtotals; use the Data Validation feature to validate data entered in cells; use database functions to summarize list values that meet the criteria you specify; and use data forms to add data.

* Use the PivotTable and PivotChart Wizard to create a PivotTable for analyzing and comparing large amounts of data; change PivotTable view by moving fields and by hiding and showing details; improve the appearance of a PivotTable by changing its field settings and applying a format; and create a PivotChart to graphically display data from a PivotTable.

* Export data from Excel to a text file, and import data from a text file into an Excel workbook; import XML data into a workbook, and export data from a workbook to an XML data file; and use Microsoft Query and the Web query feature to import data from external databases.

* Use the Goal Seek and Solver utilities to meet a target output for a formula by adjusting the values in the input cells; install and use Analysis ToolPak to perform statistical analysis; create scenarios to save various sets of input values that produce different results; and create views to save different sets of worksheet display and print settings.

* Run a macro to perform tasks automatically; record macros to perform repetitive tasks; assign a macro to a button, and use the button to run the macro; edit a macro by editing VBA code; and create a custom function to perform calculations when built-in functions are not available.

* Publish a worksheet as an interactive Web page; republish a Web page; change the source data; publish a PivotTable as a Web page; and add fields to a PivotTable after publishing it by using a Web browser.

* Use SharePoint services to create shared workspaces; view lists on the SharePoint server; and synchronize lists with data on the SharePoint server.

Skills inventory

Use the following form to gauge your skill level entering the class. For each skill listed, rate your familiarity from 1 to 5, with five being the most familiar. *This is not a test.* Rather, it is intended to provide you with an idea of where you're starting from at the beginning of class. If you're wholly unfamiliar with all the skills, you might not be ready for the class. If you think you already understand all of the skills, you might need to move on to the next course in the series. In either case, you should let your instructor know as soon as possible.

Skill	1	2	3	4	5
Defining and applying names					
Using the IF, SUMIF, and ROUND functions					
Using the PMT function					
Using the VLOOKUP, MATCH, and INDEX functions					
Using data tables to project values					
Creating automatic subtotals					
Validating data					
Using database functions					
Using data forms					
Creating, rearranging, and formatting PivotTables					
Creating PivotCharts					
Importing data from and exporting data to text files					
Importing and exporting XML data					
Using Microsoft Query and Web query					
Using Goal Seek and Solver					
Installing and using the Analysis ToolPak					
Creating scenarios and views					
Running and recording a macro					
Editing VBA modules					
Creating custom functions					
Publishing a PivotTable as an interactive Web page					
Creating Document Workspaces					
Viewing and synchronizing lists with data on a SharePoint server					

Topic C: Re-keying the course

If you have the proper hardware and software, you can re-key this course after class. This section explains what you'll need in order to do so, and how to do it.

Computer requirements

To re-key this course, your personal computer must have:

- A keyboard and a mouse
- Pentium 233 MHz processor (or higher)
- At least 128 MB RAM
- At least 400 MB of available hard drive space
- CD-ROM drive
- SVGA monitor (800×600 minimum resolution support)
- Internet access, if you want to download the Student Data files from www.courseilt.com, and for downloading the latest updates and service packs from www.windowsupdate.com

Setup instructions to re-key the course

Before you re-key the course, you will need to perform the following steps.

1   Install Microsoft Windows 2000 Professional on an NTFS partition according to the software manufacturer's instructions. Then, install the latest critical updates and service packs from www.windowsupdate.com. (You can also use Windows XP Professional, although the screen shots in this course were taken using Windows 2000, so your screens might look somewhat different.)

2   Adjust your computer's display properties as follows:

   a   Open the Control Panel and double-click Display to open the Display Properties dialog box.

   b   On the Settings tab, change the Colors setting to True Color (24 bit or 32 bit) and the Screen area to 800 by 600 pixels.

   c   On the Appearance tab, set the Scheme to Windows Classic.

   d   Click OK. If you are prompted to accept the new settings, click OK and click Yes. Then, if necessary, close the Display Properties dialog box.

3   Adjust your computer's Internet settings as follows:

   a   On the desktop, right-click the Internet Explorer icon and choose Properties to open the Internet Properties dialog box.

   b   On the Connections tab, click Setup to start the Internet Connection Wizard.

   c   Click Cancel. A message box will appear.

   d   Check "Do not show the Internet Connection wizard in the future" and click Yes.

   e   Re-open the Internet Properties dialog box.

   f   On the General tab, click Use Blank, click Apply, and click OK.

4   Install Microsoft Office 2003 according to the software manufacturer's instructions, as follows:

   a   When prompted for the CD key, enter the 25-character code included with your software.

   b   Select the Custom installation option and click Next.

   c   Clear all check boxes except Microsoft Excel.

   d   Select "Choose advanced customization of applications" and click Next.

   e   Next to Microsoft Office Excel for Windows, click the drop-down arrow and choose Run all from My Computer.

   f   Next to Office Shared Features, click the drop-down arrow and choose Run all from My Computer.

   g   Click Next. Then, click Install to start the installation.

   h   When the installation has completed successfully, click Finish.

5   At the root of the hard drive, create a Student Data folder (C:\Student Data).

6   If necessary, download the Student Data files for the course. (If you do not have an Internet connection, you can ask your instructor for a copy of the data files on a disk.)

   a   Connect to www.courseilt.com/instructor_tools.html.

   b   Click the link for Microsoft Excel 2003 to display a page of course listings, and then click the link for Excel 2003: Advanced, 2nd Edition.

   c   Click the link for downloading the Student Data files, and follow the instructions that appear on your screen.

7   Copy the data files to the Student Data folder.

8   Start Excel. Then, turn off the Office Assistant as follows:

   a   If the Office Assistant is not displayed, choose Help, Show the Office Assistant.

   b   Right-click the Office Assistant and choose Options to open the Office Assistant dialog box.

   c   Clear Use the Office Assistant and click OK.

9   Install the Solver add-in.

   a   Choose Tools, Add-Ins to open the Add-Ins dialog box.

   b   Check Solver Add-in.

   c   Click OK. If a message box prompts you to install the feature, click Yes.

10 Change the macro security level to Low.

   a   Choose Tools, Macro, Security.

   b   Select Low.

   c   Click OK.

11 Verify that Microsoft Query is installed.

   a   Choose Data, Import External Data, New Database Query.

   b   If the Choose Data Source dialog box appears, click Cancel. If Microsoft Query is not installed, a message box will prompt you to install it. Click Yes.

   c   After installation, the Choose Data Source dialog box will appear. Click Cancel to close it.

12 Dock the Formatting toolbar below the Standard toolbar.

13 If the Language bar is displayed, hide it. To do so, right-click the Language bar and choose Close the Language bar. Then, click OK.

14 If the Getting Started task pane is not displayed, choose View, Task Pane.

15 Set Excel's default file location to C:\Student Data.

    a Choose Tools, Options to open the Options dialog box.

    b Activate the General tab.

    c In the Default file location box, enter C:\Student Data.

    d Click OK.

16 Reset any other default settings in Excel that you have changed.

17 Close Excel.

CertBlaster test preparation for Microsoft Office Specialist certification

If you are interested in attaining Microsoft Office Specialist certification, you can download CertBlaster test preparation software for Excel 2003 from our Web site. Here's what you do:

1 Go to www.courseilt.com/certblaster.

2 Click the link for Excel 2003.

3 Save the .EXE file to a folder on your hard drive. (**Note**: If you skip this step, the CertBlaster software will not install correctly.)

4 Click Start and choose Run.

5 Click Browse and then navigate to the folder that contains the .EXE file.

6 Select the .EXE file and click Open.

7 Click OK and follow the on-screen instructions. When prompted for the password, enter **c_excel**.

Unit 1

Working with advanced formulas

Unit time: 45 minutes

Complete this unit, and you'll know how to:

A Use names to make your formulas easier to understand.

B Use the IF and SUMIF functions to calculate a value based on specified criteria.

C Use the nested IF function to evaluate complex conditions, and use the ROUND function to round off numbers.

D Use the PMT function to calculate periodic payments for a loan.

Topic A: Using names

This topic covers the following Microsoft Office Specialist exam objective.

#	Objective
XL03E-1-14	Define, modify and use named ranges
	• Naming one or more cell ranges
	• Using a named range reference in a formula

What's in a name?

Explanation

A *name* is a meaningful description that you assign to a cell or range of cells. After a name has been assigned, you can use it in formulas in place of cell references, making your formulas easier to understand. For example, in the formula =SUM(Qtr1), Qtr1 is the name assigned to the range of cells representing Quarter 1 data. You can use the Create Names command and the Apply Names command to assign names to cells.

Defining names for cells or ranges

Names must begin with a letter or an underscore and cannot include spaces. To define names:

1   Select the cell or range that you want to name.

2   Choose Insert, Name, Define to open the Define Name dialog box.

3   In the Names in workbook box, enter the name of the range.

4   In the Refers to box, specify the cell reference of the range that you want to name. You can also define a name in a worksheet by selecting the cells to be named and then entering the name in the Name box.

5   Click Add.

You can also define names that refer to the same cell or a range of cells across multiple worksheets. These names are called *3-D names*.

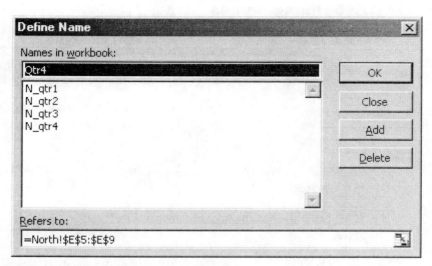

Exhibit 1-1: The Define Name dialog box

A-1:   Defining names

Here's how	Here's why
1 Start Microsoft Office Excel 2003	Click Start, and choose Programs, Microsoft Office, Microsoft Office Excel 2003.
2 Open Names	(From the current unit folder.) You'll define names to represent ranges in this workbook. You'll also use these names in formulas.
3 Save the workbook as **My names**	In the current unit folder.
Verify that the North sheet is activated	
4 Select B5:B9	You'll name this range as N_qtr1.
Edit the Name box to read **N_qtr1**	

N_qtr1	▼	*fx*	534
	A		

	(The Name box is located at the left edge of the Formula bar.) The "N" represents the North data.
Press (↵ ENTER)	To name the selected range N_qtr1.
5 Name C5:C9 as **N_qtr2**	Use the Name box. Press Enter to name the range.
Name D5:D9 as **N_qtr3**	
Name E5:E9 as **N_qtr4**	
6 Choose **Insert**, **Name**, **Define...**	To open the Define Name dialog box. The names you defined appear in the Names in workbook list, as shown in Exhibit 1-1. Now, you'll define 3-D names.
Edit the Names in workbook box to read **Qtr1_sales**	You'll define a 3-D name (Qtr1_sales) that refers to B10 across the worksheet range North:West.
In the Refers to box, delete the reference	If necessary.

7 Click

(The Collapse Dialog button is to the right of the Refers to box.) To collapse the Define Name dialog box.

Click the **North** sheet tab

To specify the first worksheet to be referenced.

While holding (SHIFT), click the **West** sheet tab

To specify the last worksheet to be referenced in the range North:West.

Select B10

To specify the cell to be referenced across the specified worksheet range.

Click

(The Expand Dialog button is to the right of the Refers to box.) To expand the Define Name dialog box.

8 Click **Add**

To add Qtr1_sales to the Names in workbook list. This name will not appear in the Name box because it is a 3-D range, which refers to multiple worksheets.

9 Define the name **Qtr2_sales** referring to C10 across North:West

Remember to click Add after defining the name.

Define the name **Qtr3_sales** referring to D10 across North:West

Define the name **Qtr4_sales** referring to E10 across North:West

Click **OK**

To close the Define Name dialog box.

10 Update the workbook

The Create Names command

Explanation

You can use the existing column and row labels as names for the cells they represent. To create names by using existing labels:

1   Select the range or ranges you want to name, including the row or column labels. The cells containing the row or column labels won't be included in the named range. They are selected to provide the appropriate labels.

2   Choose Insert, Name, Create to open the Create Names dialog box.

3   Specify the locations of the labels in the selected range.

4   Click OK.

Exhibit 1-2: The Create Names dialog box

Do it! ## A-2: Using the Create Names command

Here's how	Here's why
1 Activate the Product sales sheet	
2 Select A5:E9	By using the labels in the range A5:A9, you'll name the respective rows in the range B5:E9. For example, B5:E5 will use the label Anise Seeds.
Choose **Insert**, **Name**, **Create...**	To open the Create Names dialog box, as shown in Exhibit 1-2. Left column is checked because the selected range contains labels in the left column.
Click **OK**	To close the dialog box, creating a name for each row in the range B5:E9.
3 Select B5:E5	The name of the selected range appears as Anise_Seeds. Excel adds an underscore to the label to make the name conform to the naming conventions.
4 Observe the names of the ranges B6:E6, B7:E7, B8:E8, and B9:E9	Select a range and observe the Name box.
5 Name cells B5:E9 by using the top row labels	(Select cells B4:E9 and choose Insert, Name, Create to open the Create Names dialog box. Then, click OK.) If you don't select the top row labels (B4:E4), names will not be created.
Verify that names have been created	(Click the Name box's drop-down arrow.) You should see the names North, South, East, and West in the list.
6 Update the workbook	

The Apply Names command

Explanation
You can create several names simultaneously by using the Apply Names command. When you do so, Excel uses the labels above or to the left of columns or rows as names for those ranges. To apply names:

1   Choose Insert, Name, Apply to open the Apply Names dialog box.
2   From the Apply names list, select the names you want to apply.
3   Click OK.

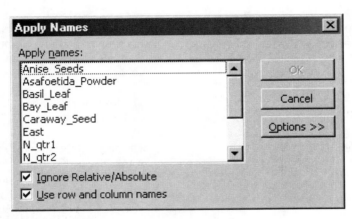

Exhibit 1-3: The Apply Names dialog box

Using a named range reference in a formula

You can use a named range in a formula to make the formula easier to understand. For example, =SUM (Qtr1_Sales) is more readily identifiable than =SUM (B3:B15). After a cell or range of cells has been named, you can substitute the name for the cell address in a formula.

Do it!   **A-3:   Using the Apply Names command**

Here's how	**Here's why**
1 Activate the North sheet	
2 Select B10	
Observe the Formula bar	f_x =SUM(B5:B9)
	The argument in the formula is the range B5:B9.
Observe the formulas for C10, D10, and E10	These SUM formulas follow the same basic pattern as B10.
3 Choose **Insert**, **Name**, **Apply...**	To open the Apply Names dialog box, as shown in Exhibit 1-3.
From the Apply names list, select the names as shown	Apply names: Bay_Leaf Caraway_Seed East N_qtr1 N_qtr2 N_qtr3 N_qtr4 North
	You don't need to press the Shift key to select multiple names. You can simply click the individual names to select them.
Click **OK**	To close the dialog box and apply these names.
4 Select B10	f_x =SUM(N_qtr1)
	In the formula bar, the range has been replaced by the name N_qtr1.
Observe the formulas for C10, D10, and E10	The SUM formulas use names instead of cell references.
5 Update and close the workbook	

Topic B: Using decision-making functions

This topic covers the following Microsoft Office Specialist exam objective.

#	Objective
XL03S-2-4	Creating formulas using the following function categories: Statistical, Date and Time, Financial, and Logical (e.g., Sum, Min, Max, Date or Now, PMT, IF, Average)
	This objective is also covered in:
	• Topic D of this unit
	• *Excel 2003: Basic*, in the unit titled "Using functions"
	• *Excel 2003: Intermediate*, in the unit titled "Advanced Formatting."

The IF function

Explanation

The IF function evaluates a condition. If the condition is true, the function returns a specific value. Otherwise, it returns another value. The syntax of the IF function is:

```
IF(condition,value_if_true,value_if_false)
```

In this syntax, `condition` is the criterion you want the function to evaluate, `value_if_true` is the value to be returned if the condition is true, and `value_if_false` is the value to be returned if the condition is false.

IF (AND

IF (OR

IF (NOT

Do it!

B-1: Using the IF function

Here's how	Here's why
1 Open Advanced formulas	This workbook contains five worksheets.
2 Save the workbook as **My advanced formulas**	In the current unit folder.
Verify that the If sheet is activated	
3 Select G7	You'll use the IF function to calculate the commission for each salesperson. If the total sales value is greater than $10,000, the commission should be calculated as 2% of the total sales. Otherwise, "Not applicable" should appear in the cell.
Type **=IF(F7>10000,**	In this function, "F7>10000" is the condition that will be evaluated.
Type **F7*2%,**	"F7*2%" is the value to be returned if the condition is true.
Type **"Not applicable")**	"Not applicable" is the value to be returned if the condition is false.
Press ↵ ENTER	The value $249 appears in G7. Because the condition F7 ($12,450)>10000 is true, the value F7*2% is returned.
4 Copy the formula in G7 to G8:G21	(Use the fill handle.) To calculate the remaining commissions.
Observe the Commission column	You'll see the commission amount for each salesperson.
5 Update the workbook	

The SUMIF function

Explanation

You use the SUMIF function when you want to add values within a range of cells based on the evaluation of a criterion in another range.

The syntax of the SUMIF function is:

```
SUMIF(evaluation_range,evaluation_criteria,sum_range)
```

In this syntax, `evaluation_range` is the range in which the function will test the criterion specified in `evaluation_criteria`. The argument `sum_range` specifies the actual cells whose values are to be added.

Do it!

B-2: Using the SUMIF function

Here's how	Here's why
1 Activate the SumIf sheet	
2 Select B29	You'll sum up the sales for the East region for the year 2003.
Type **=SUMIF(Region,**	In the formula, "Region" is the named range of cells B8:B22, which SUMIF will evaluate.
Type **"East",**	"East" is the evaluation criterion. You must include quotes around this value because it is a label.
Type **Sales_03)**	"Sales_03" is the range C8:C22, which will be summed based on the criterion.
Press ⏎ ENTER	The East region's total sales for the year 2003, $43,685.00, appears in B29.
3 In B30, display the East region's total sales for 2004	(Use the name of the range D8:D22, Sales_04, in the SUMIF function.) The value $56,320.00 appears.
In E29, display the North region's total sales for 2003	(Specify the evaluation criterion as North.) The value $65,040.00 appears.
In E30, display the North region's total sales for 2004	The value $70,950.00 appears.
4 Update the workbook	

Topic C: Creating nested functions

This topic covers the following Microsoft Office Specialist exam objective.

#	Objective
XL03E-1-13	Using Evaluate formulas

What's a nested function?

Explanation

You can use nested functions to perform complex calculations. *Nested functions* use a function as an argument of another function. For example, an IF function can contain other IF functions as arguments. You can nest up to seven levels of functions in a single formula. Excel also provides other functions, such as ROUND, to round off a number to its nearest decimal place.

Nested IF functions

You use the nested IF function to evaluate multiple conditions. For example, use a second IF function as the value_if_false argument of the first IF function.

Do it!

C-1: Using nested IF functions

Here's how	Here's why
1 Activate the Nested If sheet	
Observe the text box in the worksheet	

Sales	Commission
Below 5000	None
Between 5000-15000	1%
Between 15000-25000	1.5%
Above 25000	2%

It contains several sales ranges along with their respective commission rates.

2 Select C7	You'll calculate commissions based on the total sales and the various commission rates.
Type **=IF(B7>25000, B7*2%,**	The first IF function is applied when the total sales value in B7 is greater than 25000. If this is true, the commission is calculated as 2% of the total sales.
Type **IF(B7>15000, B7*1.5%,**	If the first condition (B7>25000) is false, this condition (B7>15000) is evaluated. If it is true, the commission is calculated as 1.5% of the total sales.
Type **IF(B7>5000, B7*1%, 0)))**	If both the first condition (B7>25000) and the second condition (B7>15000) are false, this condition (B7>5000) is evaluated. If this condition is true, the commission is calculated as 1% of total sales. If this final condition is false, 0 is returned.
Press (↵ ENTER)	Because B7 (12450) is greater than 5000. A 1% commission is calculated, and the value $124.50 appears in C7.
3 Copy the formula in C7 to C8:C21	To calculate the remaining commissions.
4 Update the workbook	

The ROUND function

Explanation

You can round off a value to a specified number of digits by using the ROUND function. The syntax of the ROUND function is:

```
ROUND(value,num_digits)
```

The first argument of the function is the value you want to round off. The second argument is the number of digits to which you want to round off that value. If `num_digits` is positive, the function rounds off the number to the specified number of decimal places. However, if `num_digits` is negative, the function rounds off the value to the left of the decimal point. For example, ROUND(126.87,1) returns 126.9, and ROUND(126.87,-1) returns 130.

Evaluation order of conditions

You might want to view the evaluation order of the conditions in a function to understand that function. To view the evaluation order:

1 Select the cell containing the function you want to evaluate. You can evaluate only one cell at a time.
2 Choose Tools, Formula Auditing, Evaluate Formula to open the Evaluate Formula dialog box.
3 Click Step In to view the value in the selected cell.
4 Click Step Out to return to the function.
5 Click Evaluate to evaluate the underlined part of the function.
6 Click Close.

use round function for division and percentages

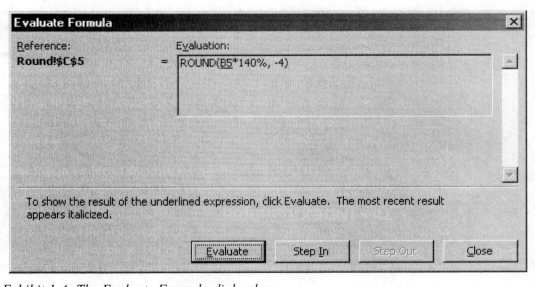

Exhibit 1-4: The Evaluate Formula dialog box

C-2: Using the ROUND function

Here's how	Here's why
1 Activate the Round sheet	
2 Select C5	You'll calculate the target sales for Atlanta.
Enter **=B5*140%**	The target sales figure for the year 2005 is calculated as 140% of the total sales in 2003. The value $9,778,688.92 appears. You'll round off the value in this cell.
3 Edit C5 to read **=ROUND(B5*140%,-4)**	In this formula, "B5*140%" is the value to be rounded, and "-4" specifies that four digits to the left of the decimal point should be rounded. In other words, the value should be rounded to the ten-thousandth place.
Press (↵ ENTER)	The value $9,780,000.00 appears.
4 Copy the formula in C5 to C6:C18	To round off the target sales values for the remaining cities.
5 Select C5	In what order is the ROUND function evaluated?
6 Choose **Tools**, **Formula Auditing**, **Evaluate Formula**	(To open the Evaluate Formula dialog box, as shown in Exhibit 1-4.) The ROUND function appears in the Evaluation box. In the function, B5 is underlined, indicating that the value in this cell is used to evaluate the function.
Click **Step In**	(To view the current value in B5.) The current value in B5 is $6,984,777.80.
Click **Step Out**	 Evaluation: = ROUND(*6984777.8**140%, -4)
	(To return to the formula.) In the formula, B5 is replaced by its current value. Notice that 140% is underlined, indicating that it will be evaluated next.

7 Click **Evaluate**	In the formula, 1.4 replaces 140%. The first argument of the ROUND function is underlined, indicating that it will be evaluated next.
Click **Evaluate**	The result of evaluation, 9778688.92, appears. The entire ROUND function is underlined. This indicates that the value 9778688.92 will be rounded off next.
Click **Evaluate**	The value $9,780,000.00 appears.
8 Click **Close**	To close the Evaluate Formula dialog box.
9 Update the workbook	

Topic D: Using financial functions

This topic covers the following Microsoft Office Specialist exam objective.

#	Objective
XL03S-2-4	Creating formulas using the following function categories: Statistical, Date and Time, Financial, and Logical (e.g., Sum, Min, Max, Date or Now, PMT, IF, Average)
	This objective is also covered in:
	• Topic B of this unit
	• *Excel 2003: Basic*, in the unit titled "Using functions"
	• *Excel 2003: Intermediate*, in the unit titled "Advanced Formatting"

A variety of functions

Explanation

Excel provides several financial functions for calculating values such as depreciation, future or present loan values, and loan payments. One financial function is the PMT function, which you can use to calculate loan payments.

The PMT function

The PMT function returns the periodic payments for a loan. The return value is negative if the amount is to be paid, and positive if the amount is to be obtained. The syntax of the PMT function is:

```
PMT(interest_rate,no_of_payments,present_val,future_val,type)
```

The following table describes each argument of the PMT function:

Argument	Description
interest_rate	The interest rate per period. For example, if you obtain a loan at 10% annual interest and make monthly payments, the first argument will be 10%/12.
no_of_payments	The number of payments that have to be made to repay the loan. For example, if you have four years to pay back the loan, and you make monthly payments, the second argument will be 48 (4*12).
present_val	The present value or the principal amount of the loan. This argument can also have a negative value. For example, if you give a loan of $12,000, then the present value will be -12000. However, if you take a loan of $12,000, then the present value will be 12000.
future_val	(Optional.) The future value of the loan—that is, its value after the last payment is made. If you omit the future value, it's assumed to be zero.
Type	(Optional.) Indicates when payments are due. This argument can have either of two values: 0 if payments are due at the end of the period, or 1 if payments are due at the beginning of the period. If you omit this argument, it's assumed to be zero.

Do it!   **D-1:   Using the PMT function**

Here's how	Here's why
1 Activate the PMT sheet	
2 Select E6	You'll calculate the monthly payment to be made to AmericaBank.
Type **=PMT(D6%/12,**	In this formula, "D6%/12" is the monthly rate of interest.
Type **C6,B6)**	"C6" refers to the cell containing the period of repayment, and "B6" refers to the cell containing the present value of the loan.
Press (↵ ENTER)	The value -$3,417.76 appears in E6. The negative sign signifies that you have to pay this amount.
3 Copy the formula in E6 to E7:E8 and E10:E11	To calculate the monthly payments for the remaining banks.
4 Change the value in C6 to **24**	Notice the changes in monthly payment.
5 Update and close the workbook	

Unit summary: Working with advanced formulas

Topic A   In this topic, you learned how to **define names**. You learned how to use the **Create Names** command to name ranges by using existing column and row labels. You also learned how to use the **Apply Names** command to replace the cell references in formulas with names.

Topic B   In this topic, you learned how to use the **IF** function to **evaluate a condition** and return a value based on whether that condition is true or false. You also learned how to use the **SUMIF** function to **add cells within a range** based upon the evaluation of the criterion in another range.

Topic C   In this topic, you learned how to use **nested** functions to perform complex calculations. You learned that a **nested IF** function can be used to evaluate multiple conditions. You also learned how to **round off** a number by using the **ROUND** function. In addition, you learned how to view the evaluation order of the conditions in a function by using the **Evaluate Formula** dialog box.

Topic D   In this topic, you learned how to use the **PMT** function to calculate periodic payments of a loan.

Independent practice activity

1 Open Advanced formulas practice.

2 Save the workbook as **My advanced formulas practice**.

3 Define names to refer to the ranges B5:B20 and C5:C20. (*Hint:* Use the Define Names command.)

4 Apply the new names to the range B5:D21. Observe how names are used in column D.

5 Display the performance grade for each salesperson based on percent increase in sales. (Use a nested IF function.) The criteria for performance grades are given in the following table:

Increase	Grade
Above 25%	A
15%–25%	B
0%–15%	C
Below 0%	D

6 Activate the Loan statement worksheet and calculate the quarterly amount to be paid to all the institutions. (*Hint:* You'll need to divide the interest rate by four instead of twelve.)

7 Compare your results with Exhibit 1-5.

8 Update and close the workbook.

	A	B	C	D	E
1			**Outlander Spices**		
2			**Statement of loan**		
3					
4	**Institution**	**Loan amount (in $)**	**Period of repayment (in quarters)**	**Annual Rate of Interest (in %)**	**Quarterly payment**
5	AmericaBank	$150,000	12	14	-$15,522.59
6	NewCiti	$325,000	16	15	-$27,379.57
7	StandardBank	$375,000	20	10	-$24,055.17
8	DoubleMoney	$450,000	20	15	-$32,382.94
9	WACA	$635,000	24	10	-$35,504.64
10	**Total**	$1,935,000			

Exhibit 1-5: The Loan statement worksheet after Step 5 of the Independent Practice Activity

Review questions

1 What is a name?

2 Names must begin with a letter or an underscore and can include spaces. True or False?

3 What command can you use to create several names simultaneously?

4 What is the advantage of using a named cell or range in a formula?

5 What is the syntax of the IF function?

6 What is a nested function?

7 If you want to view the evaluation order of a complex function, you can use the Evaluate Formula dialog box. What menu choice opens this dialog box?

8 What function returns the periodic payments for a loan?

Unit 2

Lookups and data tables

Unit time: 50 minutes

Complete this unit, and you'll know how to:

A Use the VLOOKUP function to find a value in a worksheet list.

B Use the MATCH function to find the relative position of a value in a range, and use the INDEX function to find the value of a cell at a given position within a range.

C Use data tables to project values.

Topic A: Working with lookup functions

This topic covers the following Microsoft Office Specialist exam objective.

#	Objective
XL03E-1-9	Using Lookup and Reference functions (e.g., HLOOKUP, VLOOKUP) (This objective is also covered in Topic B.)

What's a lookup function?

Explanation

You can find a value in a range of related data in a worksheet by using *lookup functions*. These functions find a lookup value in the first row or column of a list and then return a corresponding value from another row or column.

HLOOKUP and VLOOKUP

The following list describes the HLOOKUP and VLOOKUP functions:

- HLOOKUP — A horizontal lookup finds values in a lookup table that has column labels.
- VLOOKUP — A vertical lookup finds values in a lookup table that has row labels.

HLOOKUP searches for the lookup value in the first row of the lookup table and returns a value in the same column from the specified row of the table. The syntax is:

`HLOOKUP(lookup_value,table_array,row_index_num,range_lookup)`

In this syntax:

- `lookup_value` is located in the first row of the lookup table.
- `table_array` is the name of the lookup table range.
- `row_index_num` is the number of the row from which a value will be returned.
- `range_lookup` is an optional argument that specifies whether you want HLOOKUP to find an exact or approximate match. You can specify FALSE if you want the function to search for a value that falls within a range, or specify TRUE if you want the function to search for an approximate match. If you omit the argument, HLOOKUP assumes that the value is TRUE.

Similarly, VLOOKUP searches for the lookup value in the first column of the lookup table and returns a value in the same row from the specified column of the table. The syntax is:

`VLOOKUP(lookup_value,table_array,col_index_num,range_lookup)`

In this syntax:

- `lookup_value` is located in the first column of the lookup table.
- `table_array` is the name of the lookup table range.
- `col_index_num` is the number of the column from which a value will be returned.
- `range_lookup` is an optional argument that specifies whether you want VLOOKUP to find an exact or approximate match. If you omit the argument, VLOOKUP assumes that the value is TRUE.

Do it!

A-1: Examining VLOOKUP

Here's how	Here's why
1 Open Lookups	(From the current unit folder.) This workbook contains six worksheets; Lookup is the active sheet. The data in the Lookup worksheet is sorted in ascending order by the values in the Employee ID column. The range A4:E6 contains a search box that currently displays the name and department for the employee identification number E001.
2 Save the workbook as **My lookups**	In the current unit folder.
3 In A6, enter **E037**	The name and department details of Employee ID E037 appear in B6 and C6, respectively. Entering an incorrect identification number would create errors in B6 and C6.
4 Select B6	It contains a VLOOKUP function that finds the name of the employee whose identification number is specified in A6.
Observe the Formula bar	f_x =VLOOKUP(A6,Emp_info,2,FALSE)
	In this formula, "A6" refers to the cell containing the value that the function has to find. "Emp_info" is the range A10:F49, which constitutes the lookup table. The "2" refers to the table column from which the matching value is returned. "FALSE" indicates that the function must find an exact match.
	In the row containing E037, the value in the second column of the lookup table is Davis Lee.
5 Select C6	f_x =VLOOKUP(A6,Emp_info,5,FALSE)
	It contains a VLOOKUP function that finds the department of the person whose employee identification number appears in A6.
6 Update the workbook	

Use VLOOKUP for an exact match

Explanation   The following are important points related to the VLOOKUP function:

- The lookup value must always be located in the first column of the lookup table.
- If the range_lookup argument is TRUE, the values in the first column of the lookup range must be in ascending order.
- Uppercase and lowercase text are equivalent.

Do it!   ## A-2:   Using VLOOKUP for an exact match

Here's how	Here's why
1 Select D6	You'll use the VLOOKUP function to find the earnings of the employee whose ID is entered in A6.
Enter **=VLOOKUP(A6,Emp_info,6,FALSE)**	
	The value 73500 appears.
2 In E6, enter **=VLOOKUP(A6,Emp_info,4,FALSE)**	
	The value East appears. This is the region of the employee whose ID is entered in A6.
3 In A6, enter **E029**	The name, department, earnings, and region of Employee ID E029 appear in the corresponding cells.
4 Update the workbook	

Use VLOOKUP for an approximate match

Explanation

You can also use the VLOOKUP function to return an approximate match. To do this, specify the range_lookup argument as TRUE. If the function doesn't find an exact match, it looks for the largest value that is less than the lookup value and returns its corresponding data. This is also the default value if you leave the argument blank.

If the lookup value is less than the smallest value in the table, an error (#N/A) is returned.

Do it!

A-3:   Using VLOOKUP for an approximate match

Here's how	Here's why
1 Activate the Vlookup sheet	The data in this worksheet is sorted in ascending order by amount.
2 Select B6	You'll use the VLOOKUP function to find the discount percentage for the amount entered in A6.
Enter **=VLOOKUP(A6,Tran_info,2,TRUE)**	The value 10% appears in B6. The value 76,000 doesn't appear in the lookup table. Therefore, the VLOOKUP function finds the largest value that's less than that and returns the corresponding data from the specified column. The TRUE value in the last argument of the function tells VLOOKUP to look for an approximate match instead of an exact match.
3 In A6, enter **48000**	The value in B6 changes to 5%, which is the discount percentage corresponding to the amount $48,000.
4 Update the workbook	

Topic B: Using MATCH and INDEX

This topic covers the following Microsoft Office Specialist exam objective.

#	Objective
XL03E-1-9	Using Lookup and Reference functions (e.g., HLOOKUP, VLOOKUP) (This objective is also covered in Topic A.)

Two reference functions

Explanation

The MATCH and INDEX functions are considered Reference functions. You can use the MATCH function to determine the relative position of a value in a range. Conversely, the INDEX function returns a cell's value based on its relative position within a range. You can combine these two functions to obtain any information from any table.

The MATCH function

The syntax of the MATCH function is:

    MATCH(lookup_value,lookup_array,match_type)

In this syntax:

- `lookup_value` — Is the value you want to find.
- `lookup_array` — Is the range of cells containing possible lookup values.
- `match_type` — Is an optional argument that can have the values 0, 1, or -1. If you want an exact match, specify 0. If you want the function to search for the largest value that is less than or equal to the lookup value, specify 1. If you want the function to search for the smallest value that is greater than or equal to the lookup value, specify -1. If you specify 1, the range should be sorted in ascending order. If you specify -1, the range should be sorted in descending order. If you omit the argument, the function assumes that the value is 1.

Do it!

B-1: Using the MATCH function

Here's how	Here's why
1 Activate the Match sheet	The data appears in ascending order of earnings. You'll use the MATCH function to find the relative position of a value in the selected range. The ranges A4:B6 and E4:F6 contain search boxes.
2 Select B6	You'll find the relative position of "Adam Long" within the column of names.
Enter **=MATCH(B5,Emp_name,0)**	(In this formula, "B5" refers to the cell containing the lookup value. "Emp_name" refers to the range A10:A49, where the function searches for the lookup value, and "0" indicates that the values in the search range should match the lookup value exactly.) The value 17 appears in B6. This is the relative position of Adam Long within the column of names. In other words, his name is the seventeenth name in the list.
3 Select F6	You'll find the relative position of the value in F5 within the range F10:F49, named Earnings.
Enter **=MATCH(F5,Earnings,1)**	(In this formula, "1" indicates that the function will find the largest value less than or equal to the lookup value.) The relative position of the value in F5 appears as 24 in F6. In other words, there are 24 values less than or equal to $100,000.
Observe the Earnings column	It doesn't contain the value $100,000. However, MATCH still displays a relative position in F6. This occurs because MATCH returns the relative position of the largest value less than or equal to $100,000.
4 Update the workbook	

The INDEX function

Explanation

You can use the INDEX function if you want to find a value in a range by specifying a row number and a column number. The syntax of the INDEX function is:

```
INDEX(range,row_num,col_num)
```

In this syntax:

- range — Is the group of cells in which to look for the value.
- row_num — Is the row from which a value is to be returned. If the specified range contains only one row, you can omit the row number.
- col_num — Is the column from which a value is to be returned. If the specified range contains only one column, you can omit the column number.

For example, INDEX(A1:F10,4,6) returns the value in row 4 and column 6 of the range A1:F10.

You can also nest the MATCH function within an INDEX function to determine the row or column number for a given value within another range. For example, you can use MATCH to return the relative position of a specific name within a column of names. Then nest that function within an INDEX function to return the phone number for that person.

Do it!   **B-2:   Using the INDEX function**

Here's how	Here's why
1 Activate the Index sheet	You'll find the employee earnings.
2 Select A6	You'll display the value in the fourth row and the sixth column of the range A10:F49.
Enter **=INDEX(Employee_info,4,6)**	
	(In this formula, "Employee_info" refers to the range A10:F49. The "4" and "6" refer to the row and column from which the function should return a value.) The value 65000 appears in A6. This is the value from the fourth row and sixth column of the specified range.
3 Select B6	You'll display the value in row 25 of the range A10:A49, named Emp_names.
Enter **=INDEX(Emp_names,25)**	(You don't need to specify the column number if the specified range contains only one column.) The value Mary Smith appears in B6. This is the value from row 25 of the specified range.
4 Select C6	You'll use the INDEX function with the MATCH function nested inside to find the earnings of Mary Smith.
Enter **=INDEX(Employee_info,MATCH("Mary Smith",Emp_names,0),6)**	
	(In this formula, the row number is returned by the nested MATCH function.) The value 104000 appears in C6. This is the value in row 25 and column 6 of the specified range.
5 Update the workbook	

Topic C: Creating data tables

Explanation

A *data table* is a range that displays the results of changing certain values in one or more formulas. The different values you want to enter in a formula are also included in the data table. A data table can have either a single variable or two variables.

One-variable data tables

You can use a one-variable data table to observe the effects of changing one variable in one or more formulas. For example, you can see how changing the interest rate affects monthly payments in the function PMT(A5%/12,36,12000). In this function, A5 is called the *input cell*, where various input values are substituted from the data table.

To create a one-variable data table:

1   Enter input values in a row or a column.

2   If you list the input values in a column, enter the formula in the cell located at the intersection of the row above the first input value and the column to the right of the input values, as shown in Exhibit 2-1. If you list the input values in a row, enter the formula in the cell located at the intersection of the column to the left of the first value and the row just below the row of input values.

3   Select the range containing the input values and the formula.

4   Choose Data, Table to open the Table dialog box.

5   If the input values are in a column, specify the input cell in the Column input cell box. If the input values are in a row, use the Row input cell box.

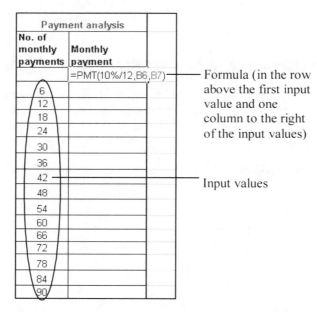

Exhibit 2-1: Creating a one-variable data table

Do it!   ## C-1:   Creating a one-variable data table

Here's how	Here's why
1 Activate the 1v data table sheet	You'll create a one-variable data table to analyze payments. D6:E21 will form the data table. D7:D21 contains the input values that you'll use while creating the data table.
2 In E6 enter **=PMT(10%/12,B6,B7)**	To calculate monthly payments based on the input cell. The value –8,791.59 appears.
3 Select D6:E21 Choose **Data, Table...**	 To open the Table dialog box. In this dialog box, you can specify the row input cell and the column input cell.
Place the insertion point in the Column input cell box Select B6	(In the worksheet.) This is the cell where the list of column input values from the data table will be substituted.
4 Click **OK**	(In the Table dialog box.) E6:E21 displays how different values for No. of monthly payments affect the monthly payment for the loan amount in B7.
5 Deselect the range	
6 Update the workbook	

Two-variable data tables

Explanation   You can use a two-variable data table to see the effect of changing two variables in one or more formulas. For example, you can see how changing the interest rate and the number of payments affects a monthly payment.

To create a two-variable data table:

1   Enter a formula that contains two input cells.

2   In the same column, below the formula, enter the first list of input values. In the same row, to the right of the formula, enter the second list of input values.

3   Select the range containing both the input values and the formula.

4   Choose Data, Table to open the Table dialog box.

5   In the Row input cell box, specify the row input cell.

6   In the Column input cell box, specify the column input cell.

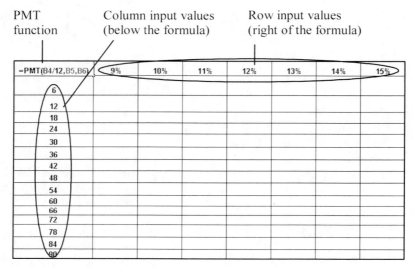

Exhibit 2-2: The two-variable data table after Step 2

Do it!   **C-2:   Creating a two-variable data table**

Here's how	**Here's why**
1 Activate the 2v data table sheet	You'll create a two-variable data table to analyze monthly payments.
2 In D4, enter **=PMT(B4/12,B5,B6)**	(As shown in Exhibit 2-2.) To calculate monthly payments based on two input cells.
3 Select D4:K19	
Open the Table dialog box	(Choose Data, Table.) The insertion point is in the Row input cell box.
4 Select B4	To specify the row input cell.
Place the insertion point in the Column input cell box	
Select B5	To specify the column input cell.
5 Click **OK**	E5:K19 displays how different numbers of months and different interest rates affect the monthly payments for the loan amount in B6.
6 In B6, enter **250000**	The data table now shows payments based on a loan amount of $250,000.
7 Update and close the workbook	

Unit summary: Lookups and data tables

Topic A   In this topic, you learned that **lookup functions** are used to find a specific value in a worksheet. You used the **VLOOKUP** function to search for a value in a list that is arranged vertically.

Topic B   In this topic, you learned how to use the **MATCH** function to find the relative position of a value in a range. You learned how to use the **INDEX** function to find a value in a range by specifying row and column numbers. You also learned how to **nest** these two functions.

Topic C   In this topic, you learned that a **data table** displays the effects of changing the values in a formula. You learned how to use a **one-variable data table** to observe the effect of changing one variable in a formula. You also learned how to use a **two-variable data table** to observe the effect of changing two variables in a formula.

Independent practice activity

1 Open Lookup practice. (Ensure that Lookup is the active worksheet.)

2 Save the workbook as **My lookup practice**.

3 In B6, enter the VLOOKUP function that finds the manager of the city entered in A6. In C6, enter the VLOOKUP function that finds the phone number of the same manager. (*Hint:* Select the range A10:C49.)

4 Activate the Index worksheet. In B6, use the MATCH and INDEX functions to find the manager of the city entered in A6. In C6, use the MATCH and INDEX functions to find the phone number of the same manager. (*Hint:* For the INDEX function, specify the range as A10:C49, and for the MATCH function, specify the range as B10:B49.)

5 Activate the 1v data table worksheet. In F6:G21, create a one-variable data table to calculate the monthly payments for the various payment schedules in F7:F21. Use the PMT function with an annual interest rate of 10%. Compare your results with Exhibit 2-3.

6 Update and close the workbook.

Payment analysis	
No. of monthly payments	Monthly deduction
	-728.55
6	-2,081.21
12	-1,066.51
18	-728.55
24	-559.78
30	-458.69
36	-391.43
42	-343.51
48	-307.67
54	-279.89
60	-257.75
66	-239.70
72	-224.74
78	-212.13
84	-201.39
90	-192.13

Exhibit 2-3: The results obtained after Step 4 of the Independent Practice Activity

Review questions

1 The VLOOKUP function is a vertical lookup function that finds values in a lookup table that has column labels. True or False?

2 What is the syntax of the VLOOKUP function?

3 List three important points to remember about the VLOOKUP function.

4 What is the purpose of the MATCH function?

5 What is a data table?

Unit 3

Advanced list management

Unit time: 45 minutes

Complete this unit, and you'll know how to:

A Summarize the data in a worksheet by creating automatic subtotals.

B Use the Data Validation feature to validate data entered in cells.

C Use database functions to summarize list values that meet the criteria you specify.

D Use data forms to add data.

Topic A: Creating subtotals

This topic covers the following Microsoft Office Specialist exam objective.

#	Objective
XL03E-1-1	Adding subtotals to worksheet data

Why subtotal?

Explanation

You can summarize data in a worksheet by calculating subtotals. You can automatically calculate subtotal and grand total values by using functions such as Sum and Average. You can also use multiple subtotals to summarize the data.

Creating subtotals in lists

If you want to create automatic subtotals, your list must contain column labels. Moreover, the list must be sorted so that the rows you want to subtotal are grouped together. For example, if you want subtotals for each region, then sort by region first to group the data. You can create subtotals for more than one type of calculation by using various summary functions, such as Sum, Max, and Min.

To create subtotals in a list:

1   Sort the list so that the rows you want to subtotal are grouped together.
2   Select any cell in the list.
3   Choose Data, Subtotal to open the Subtotal dialog box.
4   From the At each change in list, select the column that contains the groups you want subtotaled.
5   From the Use function list, select the summary function you want to use.
6   In the Add subtotal to list, check the columns for which you want subtotals.

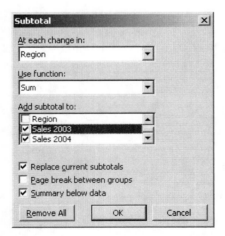

Exhibit 3-1: The Subtotal dialog box

Do it!

A-1: Creating subtotals in a list

Here's how	Here's why
1 Open List management	(From the current unit folder.) This workbook contains five worksheets, with Subtotals as the active sheet. The data are sorted by Region.
2 Save the workbook as **My list management**	In the current unit folder.
3 Select any cell in the range A4:D52	You'll calculate regional subtotals for 2003 and 2004 sales.
Choose **Data**, **Subtotals…**	To open the Subtotal dialog box. The Sum function is selected by default. Notice that Excel automatically selects the sorted list in the worksheet.
4 From the At each change in list, select **Region**	To specify the column that contains the groups for which you want subtotals.
Under Add subtotal to, check **Sales 2003**	(As shown in Exhibit 3-1.) Sales 2004 is checked by default. Sales 2003 and Sales 2004 are the columns for which you'll create subtotals.
Click **OK**	The subtotals for each region appear, along with the grand totals for all the regions. Notice that Excel outlines the data.
5 Collapse the sheet to display second-level details	

Region	Sales 2003	Sales 2004
East Total	$447,458	$407,473
North Total	$422,339	$391,866
South Total	$593,807	$596,796
West Total	$605,386	$603,545
Grand Total	$2,068,990	$1,999,680

(Click the second-level outline button.) The subtotals for all regions and the grand totals appear.

Expand the sheet to display third-level details	
6 Update the workbook	

Multiple subtotal functions

Explanation

You can also use more than one subtotal function to provide summary information. First, create a single set of subtotals based on one function. Then add the other functions one at a time. When you add a new function, be sure to clear the Replace current subtotals option in the Subtotal dialog box.

Do it!

A-2: Using multiple subtotal functions

Here's how	Here's why
1 Verify that the Subtotals sheet is activated	You'll add Max and Min subtotals to this list.
2 Select any cell in the list	(If necessary.) You'll use the Max function to create subtotals for each region.
Open the Subtotal dialog box	(Choose Data, Subtotals.) All the options you used earlier are selected.
3 From the Use function list, select **Max**	To display each region's maximum sales for the years 2003 and 2004.
Clear **Replace current subtotals**	To retain the existing subtotals.
Click **OK**	The region's maximum sales and overall maximum sales for the Sales 2003 and Sales 2004 columns appear.
4 Add minimum subtotals for the Sales 2003 and Sales 2004 columns by using the Min function	Use the Subtotal dialog box.
5 Update the workbook	

Topic B: Validating cell entries

This topic covers the following Microsoft Office Specialist exam objectives.

#	Objective
XL03E-1-4	Adding data validation criteria to cells
XL03E-1-12	Circling invalid data

What is data validation?

Explanation

You use Excel's Data Validation feature to ensure that selected cells accept only valid data, such as dates or whole numbers. You can also ensure that users select only valid values from a list.

Validating data

Validating data ensures that the entered data matches a specified format. You can display a message that prompts users for correct entries or responds to incorrect entries.

Circling invalid data

You can also specify that Excel automatically display a circle around invalid entries by clicking the Circle Invalid Data button on the Formula Auditing toolbar. To hide validation circles, click the Clear Validation Circles button on the Formula Auditing toolbar.

Do it!

B-1: Observing data validation

Here's how	Here's why
1 Activate the Observing data validation sheet	You'll observe the cells in which only certain kinds of data can be entered.
2 Select B7, as shown	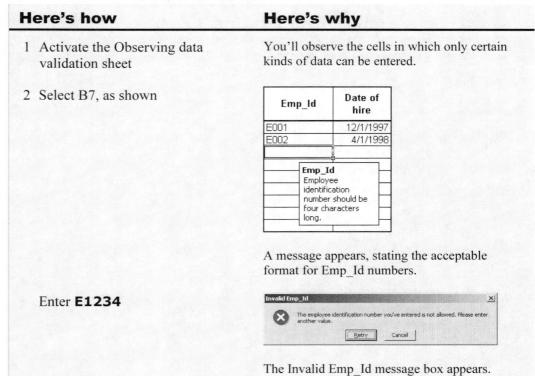 A message appears, stating the acceptable format for Emp_Id numbers.
Enter **E1234**	The Invalid Emp_Id message box appears.

3 Click **Retry**	To close the message box.
Edit B7 to read **E003**	
Press (↵ ENTER)	The cell accepts the corrected Emp_Id.
4 Select C7	
Enter tomorrow's date	(In mm/dd/yy format.) This date is not permitted because the date-of-hire value cannot be greater than today's date value. The Invalid date of hire message box appears.
Click **Retry**	
5 Enter today's date	The cell accepts the corrected date.
6 Select D7	A drop-down arrow appears.
Enter **Sales**	An error message box appears.
Click **Cancel**	To close the message box and clear the cell contents.
7 Click the drop-down arrow	To display the list of valid departments.
Select **National sales**	
8 Update the workbook	

Setting data validation rules

Explanation   To create a set of rules for data validation:

1 Select the cells for which you want to create a validation rule.
2 Choose Data, Validation to open the Data Validation dialog box.
3 Click the Settings tab.
4 From the Allow list, select a data validation option.
5 From the Data list, select the operator you want. Then complete the remaining entries.
6 Click OK to set the validation rule and close the dialog box.

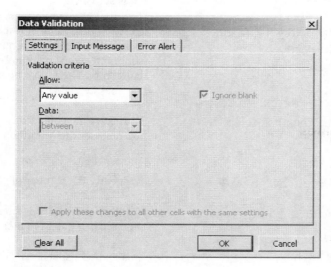

Exhibit 3-2: The Data Validation dialog box

B-2:   Setting up data validation

Here's how	Here's why
1 Activate the Setting up data validation sheet	
2 Select B5:B20	You'll create a validation rule to ensure that the employee numbers are four characters long.
Choose **Data**, **Validation...**	To open the Data Validation dialog box, as shown in Exhibit 3-2. By default, the Settings tab is activated.
From the Allow list, select **Text length**	To specify the number of characters permitted in each cell of the selected range. The Data list and Minimum and Maximum boxes appear in the dialog box. The Ignore blank option also becomes available.
From the Data list, select **equal to**	To specify the comparison operator. The Length box replaces the Minimum and Maximum boxes.
In the Length box, type **4**	To specify the number of characters permitted.
3 Activate the Input Message tab	You'll specify the input message that will appear when the user enters an invalid Emp_Id.
In the Title box, enter **Emp_Id**	This text will appear as a title in the input message.
In the Input message box, enter **Employee identification number should be four characters long.**	This message will appear when the user selects a cell.
4 Activate the Error Alert tab	
In the Title box, enter **Invalid Emp_Id**	This will be the title of the error message box.
In the Error message box, enter **The employee identification number you've entered is not permitted. Please enter another value.**	This is the error message that'll appear when the user enters an invalid employee identification number.
Click **OK**	To set the validation.
5 Observe the screen	The input message appears.
6 Select **B5**	

7	Enter **103**	The Invalid Emp_Id message box appears because you entered only three characters.
	Click **Cancel**	
	Enter **E103**	
8	Select C5:C20	You'll create a validation rule to ensure that the date of hire is on or before today's date.
	Open the Data Validation dialog box	Choose Data, Validation.
9	Activate the Settings tab	
	From the Allow list, select **Date**	
	From the Data list, select **less than or equal to**	
	In the End date box, enter **=TODAY()**	To specify the validation date as today's date.
	Click **OK**	To set the validation.
10	In C5, enter tomorrow's date	(In mm/dd/yy format.) An error message box appears.
	Click **Cancel**	
	Enter a valid date of hire	A date less than or equal to today's date.
11	Select D5:D20	You'll create a list of valid departments from which the user can choose.
	Open the Data Validation dialog box	The Settings tab is activated.
	From the Allow list, select **List**	
	In the Source box, type **Accounting, Customer support, Human resources, Marketing, National sales**	To create the list of values for the column.
	Click **OK**	(To set the validation rule.) A drop-down arrow appears to the right of D5.
12	Click the drop-down arrow	
	Select **Marketing**	
13	Update the workbook	

Topic C: Exploring database functions

This topic covers the following Microsoft Office Specialist exam objective.

#	Objective
XL03E-1-10	Creating and editing Database functions (e.g., DSUM, DAVERAGE)

What's a database?

Explanation

A *database* is a collection of related information. In a database, the rows of related data are called *records*, and the columns are called *fields*. The first row of a database contains the names of the fields. In Excel, the terms "database" and "list" mean the same thing.

You can summarize values that meet complex criteria by using database functions, such as DSUM, DCOUNT, and DAVERAGE. For example, you can use DCOUNT to find the total number of salespeople who joined the staff of a specific store in a certain year.

Structure of database functions

The syntax of a database function is:

```
Dfunction(database,field,criteria)
```

In this syntax:

- `database` is the range containing the list of related information. Each row is a record, and each column is a field. The first row of the database must contain labels for each field.

- `field` is the column to be used by the function. Here you can specify the column name, such as Emp_Id, or a number that represents the position of the column in the database.

- `criteria` is the range that contains the conditions a row must meet to be included in the calculation. The function considers only those database records that meet the specified conditions. The first row of the criteria range must include field names that correspond precisely to field names in the database. When you include more than one row in the criteria range, the new row is considered to be an "Or" condition. That is, rows will be included if they match the conditions in the first row or if they match those in subsequent rows. An Or condition will increase the number of matching rows.

The following examples are based on the database shown in Exhibit 3-3:

- DSUM(database, "Sales 2004",A2:B3) returns the total sales of Annatto Seed in the East region for the year 2004.

- DCOUNT(database,"Store code",A2:C3) returns the number of stores in the East region where total sales of Annatto Seed were less than $50,000 for the year 2004.

- DSUM(database,"Sales 2004",A2:A4) returns the total sales of Annatto Seed and Anise Seeds for the year 2004.

	A	B	C	D	E
1	Criteria				
2	Product	Region	Sales 2004		
3	Annatto Seed	East	<50,000		
4	Anise Seeds	North			
5					
6	Average sales of Annatto Seed in East for 2004				$30,479.90
7	Total sales of Annatto Seed and Anise Seeds for 2004				$623,570.92
8	Number of stores where total sales of Annatto Seed was less				4
9	than $50,000 in 2004				
10					
11	Database				
12	Product	Region	Store code	Sales 2003	Sales 2004
13	Annatto Seed	East	ES008		$24,181.04
14	Cinnamon	East	ES008	$87,970.00	$67,240.00
15	Anise Seeds	East	ES211	$11,312.31	$20,218.31
16	Annatto Seed	East	ES211	$58,842.00	$49,530.00
17	Cinnamon	East	ES211	$99,665.00	$31,705.00
18	Anise Seeds	East	ES367	$22,772.00	$57,510.00
19	Annatto Seed	East	ES367	$17,990.07	$18,157.57
20	Asafoetida Powder	East	ES367	$19,425.69	$23,273.19

Exhibit 3-3: A database function worksheet

Do it!

C-1: Examining the structure of database functions

Here's how	Here's why
1 Click as shown	⊮ ◀ ▶ ▸⎸ \ Subtotals \ Ready (The tab scrolling buttons are to the left of the sheet tabs.) To fully display the Database functions sheet tab.
2 Activate the Database functions sheet	You'll examine the structure of database functions. The blank cells in the Sales 2003 column indicate that this product was not sold by the specific store in 2003.
Select the range named **Database**	(Select Database from the Name box.) The first row in the range contains unique text labels or field names that identify the data in the columns below them.
Select the range named **Criteria**	This range specifies the conditions for the database functions. The first row contains field names that must exactly match those in the database.
3 Select E6	
Observe the Formula bar	*ƒx* =DAVERAGE(Database,"Sales 2004",A2:B3) This function calculates the average sales of Annatto Seed in the East region for the year 2004. In this formula, "Database" is the name of the range that forms the database, "Sales 2004" indicates the column to be used in the function, and "A2:B3" specifies the criteria range.
4 Select E7	
Observe the Formula bar	*ƒx* =DSUM(Database,5,A2:A4) This function sums the sales of Annatto Seed and Anise Seeds for the year 2004. In this formula, "5" represents the column on which the function will perform the calculation. You can use the column number or column name as this argument.
5 Select E8	*ƒx* =DCOUNT(Database,"Sales 2004",A2:C3) This function counts the number of stores whose total sales for the year 2004 was less than $50,000 in the East region.

The DSUM and DAVERAGE functions

Explanation   You can use the DSUM function to add only those values in a database column that meet a specified criterion. For example, you could use DSUM to calculate the total sales for a store in a specific year or for one product in a certain region. The syntax of DSUM function is:

```
DSUM(database,field,criteria)
```

You can use the DAVERAGE function to average the values in a column of a list or database that match conditions you specify. The syntax of DSUM function is:

```
DAVERAGE(database,field,criteria)
```

Do it!   ## C-2:   Using the DSUM function

Here's how	Here's why
1 Activate the DSUM sheet	
Select the range named **Db**	This range forms the database.
2 Select D5	You'll calculate the total sales of Annatto Seed and Anise Seeds of grade A quality.
Type **=DSUM(Db,**	In this formula, "Db" is the name of the range that represents the database.
Type **4,**	This indicates the column on which the function will perform the calculation. In this case, the fourth column in the database is Sales.
Type **A1:B3)**	"A1:B3" specifies the criteria range.
Press `← ENTER`	The function displays $57,850.35, which is the total sales of Annatto Seed and Anise Seeds of grade A quality.
3 Select D6	(If necessary.) You'll sum the values in the Sales column for those records of Annatto Seed where the quality grades are B, C, and D.
Type **=DSUM(Db,4,**	
Type **D1:F2)**	The criterion specifies rows in which the grade is both "greater than" A and "less than" E. For letters, this means that the character falls between A and E in alphabetical order.
Press `← ENTER`	The function displays $139,843.45, which is the total sale of Annatto Seed of grades B, C, and D quality.
4 Update the workbook	

Topic D: Working with data forms

Explanation

After you set up a list, a data form provides a simple interface for working with that list. For a data form to be created, your list must have column headings in the first row of the data range. Excel uses these headings to create a form for browsing, finding, entering, and deleting data.

Data forms

A *data form* is a dialog box that gives you an edit field for each column that doesn't contain a formula. Users can type data in these edit boxes to create new rows in the list or to edit existing rows. If one of the columns contains a formula, Excel automatically enters and calculates the formula for new data. When you complete the edit boxes in the data form, click Close to close the dialog box, or click New to add another record.

In addition to using the data form to enter data, you can perform other actions, such as finding a specific record, browsing through a list, and managing records in a list. The following table suggests ways in which you can use a data form:

Option	Description
New	Adds a new record based on the data entered in the edit fields and displays a new, blank entry form.
Delete	Deletes the displayed record.
Restore	Restores edited information until you click the New button.
Find Prev	Displays the previous record in the data form. If you enter a criterion, you'll move to the previous record that matches the criterion.
Find Next	Displays the next matching record in the data form. If you enter a criterion, you'll move to the next record that matches the criterion.
Criteria	Displays a blank form in which you can enter search criteria. You can then use the Find Prev and Find Next buttons to search for records that match the criteria.
Close	Closes the dialog box and adds data in the edit fields to the list.

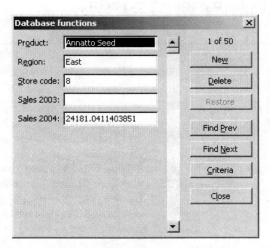

Exhibit 3-4: The Database functions dialog box

D-1: Entering data by using a form

Here's how	Here's why
1 Activate the Database functions sheet	
Select any cell in the database range	To use a data form, you must first select a cell within a valid list. The labels in row 12 will serve as the field names in the data form.
2 Choose **Data, Form...**	To open the Database functions dialog box, as shown in Exhibit 3-4. It shows the first record of the list, presented as a form. The upper-right corner displays the number of the record and the total number of records in the list. The Sales 2003 box is blank.
3 In the Sales 2003 box, type **22000**	
Press ⏎ ENTER	To enter the new data in the list and move to the next record.
Observe cell D13	(You'll need to move the data form.) The new value is entered in the list and has the proper formatting.
4 Click **New**	To create a new, blank record in the list.
Enter the data as shown	Product: Cardamom (ground) Region: North Store code: NS211 Sales 2003: 11000 Sales 2004: 32000
5 Click **Close**	To close the data form and add the new data to the list. The last row in the list now contains the data you just entered.
6 Update and close the workbook	

Unit summary: Advanced list management

Topic A   In this topic, you learned that **subtotals** summarize worksheet data. You also learned how to use **multiple subtotal functions**, such as Sum, Min, and Max, at one time.

Topic B   In this topic, you learned about the **data validation** feature of Excel. You learned that data validation ensures the entry of valid information in a worksheet. You learned how to **specify** a **set of rules** to perform data validation. You also learned that the **validation rules** display error messages to prompt the user to enter correct data.

Topic C   In this topic, you learned about **database functions**, such as **DSUM**, **DAVERAGE**, and **DCOUNT**. You learned that database functions are used to summarize data according to specific criteria. You also learned how to use the **DSUM** function to add values that meet complex criteria.

Topic D   In this topic, you learned how to use a **data form**. You learned that data forms are used to enter data, delete data, restore data, and find data in a list.

Independent practice activity

1 Open List management practice. (Ensure that the Subtotals worksheet is active.)

2 Save the workbook as **My list management practice**.

3 Create product-wise subtotals for the Sales 2003 and Sales 2004 columns by using the Sum, Average, and Max functions.

4 Activate the Data validation worksheet. Create a data validation rule to accept only those Store codes with lengths between four and six characters in the range A5:A24.

5 Create a list of regions from which users can choose for the range B5:B24. The list should contain **East**, **North**, **South**, and **West**. Also, ensure that a proper error message appears when the user enters an invalid region.

6 Create a data validation rule to ensure that the range C5:C24 accepts only whole numbers greater than zero.

7 Activate the Database functions worksheet. In H5, enter a database function that counts the total number of salespeople whose total sales were greater than $10,000 and whose sales in quarter 3 were greater than $3,000. (*Hint:* Use the DCOUNT function. Your answer should be 4.)

8 By using the data form, enter a new record, as shown in Exhibit 3-5.

9 Update and close the workbook.

Salesperson:	Anna Morris
Qtr1:	1550
Qtr2:	2220
Qtr3:	1850
Qtr4:	3150

Exhibit 3-5: The data to be entered in Step 8 of the Independent Practice Activity

Review questions

1 If you want to create automatic subtotals, what must your list contain?

2 What's the purpose of validating data?

3 List the steps you would use to set data validation rules.

4 In Excel, what is the difference between the terms "database" and "list?"

5 What is the syntax of the DSUM function?

6 What is a data form?

Unit 4

Working with PivotTables and PivotCharts

Unit time: 50 minutes

Complete this unit, and you'll know how to:

A Use the PivotTable and PivotChart Wizard to create a PivotTable for analyzing and comparing large amounts of data.

B Change PivotTable view by moving fields and by hiding and showing details.

C Improve the appearance of a PivotTable by changing its field settings and applying a format.

D Create a PivotChart to graphically display data from a PivotTable.

Topic A: Working with PivotTables

This topic covers the following Microsoft Office Specialist exam objective.

#	Objective
XL03E-1-8	Creating PivotTable Reports and PivotChart Reports (This objective is also covered in Topic D.)

What's a PivotTable?

Explanation

By analyzing data, you can make more informed decisions. Excel provides the PivotTable feature to help you examine data. A *PivotTable* is an interactive table that summarizes, organizes, and compares large amounts of data in a worksheet. You can rotate the rows and columns in a PivotTable to obtain different views of the same data. You can use a PivotTable to analyze data in an Excel workbook or from an external database, such as Microsoft Access or SQL Server.

Examining PivotTables

The data on which a PivotTable is based is called the *source data*. You add categories of information, called *fields*, to different parts of the PivotTable to determine how the data is arranged. You can add four types of fields, shown in Exhibit 4-1 and explained in the following table:

name range before creating pivot table

always use new worksheet

Field	Description
Page	Filters the summarized data in the PivotTable. If you select an item in the page field, the view of the PivotTable changes to display only the summarized data associated with that item. For example, if Region is a page field, you can display the summarized data for North, West, or all regions.
Row	Displays the items in a field as row labels. For example, in Exhibit 4-1, Quarter is a row field, which means that the table shows one row for each quarter.
Column	Displays the items in a field as column labels. For example, in Exhibit 4-1, Product is a column field, which means that the table shows one column for each product.
Data	Contains the summarized data. These fields usually contain numeric data, such as sales and inventory. The area where the data itself appears is called the *data area*.

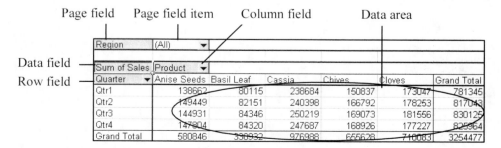

Exhibit 4-1: A sample PivotTable

The PivotTable and PivotChart Wizard

You use the PivotTable and PivotChart Wizard to create a PivotTable. To create a PivotTable:

1 Choose Data, PivotTable and PivotChart Report to start the wizard.

2 Under What kind of report do you want to create?, select PivotTable. Click Next.

3 In the Range box, select the range that contains the data to be used in the PivotTable. Click Next.

4 Select the location for the PivotTable. You can place the PivotTable in a new or existing worksheet. Click Finish to create the PivotTable and close the wizard.

Do it!

A-1:   Creating a PivotTable

Here's how	Here's why
1 Open PivotTable	(From the current unit folder.) The Pivot worksheet contains the sales details for several products. You'll use the data in this worksheet to create a PivotTable.
2 Save the workbook as **My PivotTable**	In the current unit folder.
3 Select any cell in the range A5:D105	You'll create a PivotTable based on this range. If you select a cell within the range of the source data, you don't have to specify the range later.
4 Choose **Data**, **PivotTable and PivotChart Report...**	To open Step 1 of the PivotTable and PivotChart Wizard. It prompts you to select the location of the data you want to analyze. You can use an external data source or an Excel worksheet. The wizard also prompts you to select the type of report you want to create. By default, the PivotTable option is selected.
Click **Next**	To move to Step 2 of the wizard. The Range box automatically shows the range containing the source data because you selected a cell within that range.
5 Click **Next**	To move to Step 3 of the wizard. It prompts you to specify the location of the PivotTable report. You can create the PivotTable in a new worksheet or in an existing worksheet. The default selection is New worksheet.
6 Click **Finish**	A new worksheet, Sheet1, is added to the workbook. This worksheet displays the layout of the PivotTable, the PivotTable toolbar, and the PivotTable Field List window.
7 Update the workbook	

Add fields

Explanation You can add fields to a PivotTable to specify the data you want to display. The fields of the source data appear in the PivotTable Field List window.

To add fields, drag the relevant field from the PivotTable Field List window to a suitable area in the PivotTable layout.

Do it! ## A-2: Adding fields

Here's how	Here's why
1 Verify that Sheet1 is activated	You'll add fields in the PivotTable layout.
Observe the PivotTable Field List window	It displays the column headings of the source data in the Pivot worksheet.
2 Point to **Region**	(In the PivotTable Field List window.) You'll use Region as a Page field.
Drag **Region** to Drop Page Fields Here, as shown	Region appears with a drop-down arrow.
3 Drag **Quarter** to Drop Row Fields Here, as shown	
	(Quarter is in the PivotTable Field List window.) To add Quarter as a row field in the PivotTable.
4 Drag **Product** to Drop Column Fields Here, as shown	
	To add Product as a column field.
5 Drag **Sales** to Drop Data Items Here	To add Sales as the data item. The PivotTable shows the quarterly sales for several products. You can change the view by changing the selections in the Product, Quarter, and Region lists.

6   Click as shown

Product ▼	
Anise Seeds	Basil Leaf

To display the Product list.

Clear **Basil Leaf**, **Cassia**, and **Cloves**

To specify that the only products shown will be Anise Seeds and Chives.

Click **OK**

The worksheet now shows the sales of only Anise Seeds and Chives.

7   Click as shown

A	B	
Region	(All)	▼

To display the Region list.

From the Region list, select **Central**

To specify that the view will include the sales of Anise Seeds and Chives in the Central region only.

Click **OK**

To close the list. The PivotTable displays the sales of Anise Seeds and Chives in the Central region.

8   Display data for all of the products for all the regions

Check Show All in the Product list, and select All from the Region list.

9   Update the workbook

Topic B: Rearranging PivotTables

Explanation

After creating a PivotTable, you might want to display an entirely different view of the data. You can change the data view by dragging the fields to other areas in the PivotTable. The PivotTable provides options to show or hide the details. However, to change data in the PivotTable, you need to refresh the table after changing the source data.

Move fields

You can move a field in a PivotTable by dragging the field to a new location. To show a columnar view of the data, drag a page or a row field to the column area of the PivotTable. When you want to arrange data in row fields, drag a page or a column field to the row area of the PivotTable.

Sum of Sales		Quarter				
Product	Region	Qtr1	Qtr2	Qtr3	Qtr4	Grand Total
Anise Seeds	Central	26000	33112	28874	27220	115206
	East	25617	27818	28224	31321	112980
	North	29269	29919	28433	27363	114984
	South	12776	12600	12900	13400	51676
	West	45000	46000	46500	48500	186000
Anise Seeds Total		138662	149449	144931	147804	580846
Basil Leaf	Central	13800	15080	12821	16363	58064
	East	18213	17849	18291	15345	69698
	North	16955	15532	17834	16710	67031
	South	15435	17345	18200	16982	67962
	West	15712	16345	17200	18920	68177
Basil Leaf Total		80115	82151	84346	84320	330932

Exhibit 4-2: The PivotTable after Step 4 of the following activity

Do it!   **B-1:   Moving fields**

Here's how	Here's why
1 Observe the PivotTable	It shows the quarterly sales of several products. You'll move the fields to show the data in a different way.
2 Drag **Region** as shown	
	(Drag Region from the worksheet.) You'll change Region from a page field to a row field.
3 Observe the PivotTable	The data view changes to show the sales of products by quarter within different regions.
4 Specify **Quarter** as a column field	Drag it to where Product is located.
Specify **Product** as a row field	(Drag it to the left of Region.) The rows now show the product sales for all the regions, as displayed in Exhibit 4-2.
5 Update the workbook	

Hide and show details

You can show and hide details in a PivotTable that has more than one row or column field. To hide details, select the cell or range and click the Hide Detail button on the PivotTable toolbar. To display hidden details, select the cell or range and click the Show Detail button on the PivotTable toolbar.

B-2:   Hiding and showing details

Here's how	Here's why
1 Select A5:G34	You'll hide the sales details for regions and show only the total sales for each product.
2 Click [button]	(The Hide Detail button is on the PivotTable toolbar.) To hide the regional sales details.
Deselect the range	The worksheet shows only a summary of the sales details for each region.

Sum of Sales		Quarter ▼				
Product ▼	Region ▼	Qtr1	Qtr2	Qtr3	Qtr4	Grand Total
Anise Seeds		138662	149449	144931	147804	580846
Basil Leaf		80115	82151	84346	84320	330932
Cassia		238684	240398	250219	247687	976988
Chives		150837	166792	169073	168926	655628
Cloves		173047	178253	181556	177227	710083
Grand Total		781345	817043	830125	825964	3254477

3 Select A5:G9	You'll show the details of this range.
4 Click [button]	(The Show Detail button is on the PivotTable toolbar.) To show the regional sales details for each product.
5 Update the workbook	

Refresh data

Explanation

You cannot directly change the data in a PivotTable because it's based on source data. To change data in a PivotTable, you must first change the source data and then refresh the PivotTable to reflect the latest changes. You can refresh the PivotTable by clicking the Refresh Data button on the toolbar.

Do it!

B-3:   Refreshing the data in a PivotTable

Here's how	Here's why
1 Select C5	It shows the value 26000.
Enter **30000**	When you try to enter the first character, a message box appears with a warning that you can't change the value in a PivotTable.
Click **OK**	
2 Activate the Pivot sheet	This contains the source data for the PivotTable. To change the data in the PivotTable, you have to change the values in this worksheet.
3 Select D6	The cell shows the value $26,000. You'll change this value and then view the result in the PivotTable.
Edit D6 to read **30000**	
4 Activate Sheet1	Notice that C5 still shows the old value.
5 Click	(The Refresh External Data button is on the PivotTable toolbar.) To update the PivotTable with the latest data. C5 now shows the new value.
6 Update the workbook	

Microsoft Excel: Cannot change this part of a PivotTable report. OK

Topic C: Formatting PivotTables

Explanation

You can modify the format of a PivotTable by using the PivotTable Field and AutoFormat dialog boxes. The PivotTable Field dialog box helps you change number formats, specify how data is summarized, and show or hide data. The AutoFormat dialog box makes it possible to format an entire PivotTable in one step.

Change field settings

You can change field settings to alter how data appears or is summarized in a PivotTable. To change field settings:

1   Select any cell within the data area.

2   On the PivotTable toolbar, click the Field Settings button to open the PivotTable Field dialog box.

3   Click the Number button to open the Format Cells dialog box.

4   Select the relevant options, and click OK to apply the formatting.

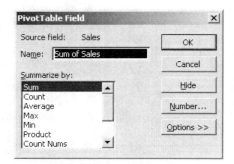

Exhibit 4-3: The PivotTable Field dialog box

Do it!   ## C-1: Changing field settings

Here's how	Here's why
1 Select C5	(If necessary.) This cell is within the data area. You'll apply a number format to the data items.
2 Click [icon]	(The Field Settings button is on the PivotTable toolbar.) To open the PivotTable Field dialog box, as shown in Exhibit 4-3.
3 Click **Number**	To open the Format Cells dialog box.
From the Category list, select **Number**	
Check **Use 1000 Separator (,)**	To display a comma at every thousandth position of the number.
4 From the Category list, select **Currency**	To view the formatting options available under Currency. The $ option is selected in the Symbol list. You'll add this prefix symbol to the sales values.
Edit the Decimal places box to read **0**	To specify that currency values should be displayed as whole-dollar amounts.
5 Click **OK**	To close the Format Cells dialog box.
Click **OK**	

Qtr1	Qtr2	Qtr3	Qtr4	Grand Total
$30,000	$33,112	$28,874	$27,220	$119,206
$25,617	$27,818	$28,224	$31,321	$112,980
$29,269	$29,919	$28,433	$27,363	$114,984
$12,776	$12,600	$12,900	$13,400	$51,676
$45,000	$46,000	$46,500	$48,500	$186,000
$142,662	$149,449	$144,931	$147,804	$584,846

To close the PivotTable Field dialog box and apply the formatting. The values are now formatted with commas and the $ symbol.

6 Update the workbook

The AutoFormat dialog box

Explanation

Click the Format Report button to open the AutoFormat dialog box. This dialog box contains a list of predefined formats that you can apply to a PivotTable. The formats are divided into two categories: Report and Table.

You can use the Report formats, Report 1 to Report 10, when you want to indent the PivotTable. These types of formats will result in a change in layout, character, and cell formats. Exhibit 4-4 shows a sample Report format.

Quarter ▾	Year ▾	Product ▾	Sales
Qtr1			**852497.358**
	2001		**123443**
		Anise Seeds	26000
		Basil Leaf	13800
		Cassia	45000
		Chives	18300
		Cloves	20343
	2002		**139490.59**
		Anise Seeds	29380
		Basil Leaf	15594
		Cassia	50850
		Chives	20679
		Cloves	22987.59
	2003		**165413.62**

Exhibit 4-4: A sample Report format

You can use the Table formats, Table1 to Table 10, when you want a PivotTable that is not indented. These formats don't change the layout of the PivotTable. Exhibit 4-5 shows a sample Table format.

Sales		Quarter ▾				
Product ▾	**Region** ▾	**Qtr1**	**Qtr2**	**Qtr3**	**Qtr4**	**Grand Total**
Anise Seed	Central	$30,000	$33,112	$28,874	$27,220	$119,206
	East	$25,617	$27,818	$28,224	$31,321	$112,980
	North	$29,269	$29,919	$28,433	$27,363	$114,984
	South	$12,776	$12,600	$12,900	$13,400	$51,676
	West	$45,000	$46,000	$46,500	$48,500	$186,000
Anise Seeds Total		**$142,662**	**$149,449**	**$144,931**	**$147,804**	**$584,846**
Basil Leaf	Central	$13,800	$15,080	$12,821	$16,363	$58,064
	East	$18,213	$17,849	$18,291	$15,345	$69,698
	North	$16,955	$15,532	$17,834	$16,710	$67,031
	South	$15,435	$17,345	$18,200	$16,982	$67,962
	West	$15,712	$16,345	$17,200	$18,920	$68,177
Basil Leaf Total		**$80,115**	**$82,151**	**$84,346**	**$84,320**	**$330,932**

Exhibit 4-5: A sample Table format

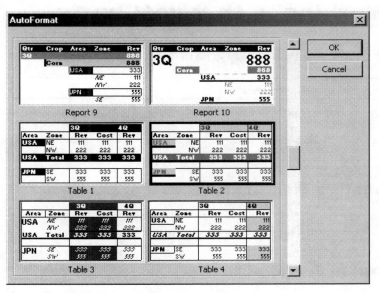

Exhibit 4-6: The AutoFormat dialog box

Do it!

C-2:   Using the AutoFormat dialog box

Here's how	Here's why
1 Click [icon]	(The Format Report button is on the PivotTable toolbar.) To open the AutoFormat dialog box, which displays previews of the available formats.
2 Select the Table 2 format	As shown in Exhibit 4-6. You'll have to scroll down to view this option.
3 Click **OK**	
Deselect the range	The Table 2 format is applied to the data.
4 Update the workbook	

Topic D: Working with PivotCharts

This topic covers the following Microsoft Office Specialist exam objective.

#	Objective
XL03E-1-8	Creating PivotTable Reports and PivotChart Reports (This objective is also covered in Topic A.)

What's a PivotChart?

Explanation

You can use a PivotChart to graphically display data from a PivotTable. A single PivotChart provides different views of the same data.

Create PivotCharts

When you create a PivotChart, the row fields of the PivotTable become the categories, and the column fields become the series.

To create a PivotChart, click the Chart Wizard button on the PivotTable toolbar. You can also right-click anywhere on the PivotTable and choose PivotChart from the shortcut menu.

Do it!   **D-1:   Creating a PivotChart**

Here's how	Here's why
1 Verify that Sheet1 is activated	You'll create a PivotChart based on the data in the PivotTable.
2 Right-click the PivotTable	(You can right-click anywhere in the table.) A shortcut menu appears.
Choose **PivotChart**	(To create a PivotChart in a separate worksheet.) The x-axis of the chart represents the products for each region. You'll change the chart to show only the total sales for each region.
3 Point to **Product**	(At the bottom of the chart.) You'll move Product to make it a page field. This will remove products from the x-axis.
Drag **Product** to Drop Page Fields Here	(To make Product a page field.) You can now sort and filter data in the PivotChart by using Product.
Observe the PivotChart	The total sales for the five regions appear in columns, and each column is divided into quarters. You can use the Product, Region, and Quarter lists to change the data represented by the PivotChart.
4 From the Product list, select **Basil Leaf**	
Click **OK**	The PivotChart displays the total sales of only Basil Leaf for all regions.
5 From the Quarter list, clear all of the options except Qtr1	
Click **OK**	This will show the total sales of Basil Leaf in the first quarter for all regions.
6 Update and close the workbook	

stop ←

Unit summary: Working with PivotTables and PivotCharts

Topic A   In this topic, you learned that a **PivotTable** is used to **summarize**, **organize**, and **compare** large amounts of data in a worksheet. You learned how to **create** a PivotTable by using the **PivotTable and PivotChart Wizard**. Then, you learned how to **add fields** to the **layout** of a PivotTable.

Topic B   In this topic, you learned how to change the appearance of data in a PivotTable by moving the **page**, **row**, and **column fields** to different areas. You also learned how to **hide** and **show details** in the PivotTable.

Topic C   In this topic, you learned how to use the **Field Settings button** to apply formatting to numerical data. You also learned how to use the **AutoFormat dialog box** to format an entire PivotTable.

Topic D   In this topic, you learned that **PivotCharts** graphically display data from the PivotTable. You also learned how to **create PivotCharts**. You learned that moving the fields in the PivotChart changes the way data is presented.

Independent practice activity

1 Open PivotTable practice.

2 Save the workbook as **My PivotTable practice**.

3 Create a PivotTable, as shown in Exhibit 4-7, based on the data in the PivotPrac worksheet.

4 Move Year to the row area, move Quarter to the column area, and move Product to the row area to the right of the Year field. Compare your results with Exhibit 4-8.

> *move sales to data area*

5 Apply the Report 6 AutoFormat to the PivotTable.

6 Create a PivotChart.

7 Make Quarter and Year page fields in the PivotChart. (*Hint:* Drag the fields to Drop Page Fields Here.)

8 Compare your results with Exhibit 4-9.

9 Change the PivotChart to display the sales in the first quarter of 2003.

10 Update and close the workbook.

Year	(All) ▼					
Sum of Sales	Product ▼					
Quarter ▼	Anise Seeds	Basil Leaf	Cassia	Chives	Cloves	Grand Total
Qtr1	179556	95302.8	310770	126379.8	140488.758	852497.358
Qtr2	228671.472	104142.48	303746.598	172884.804	165744	975189.354
Qtr3	199403.844	88541.826	320044.758	198057.174	159072.804	965120.406
Qtr4	187981.32	113002.878	316930.152	177173.43	136497.09	931584.87
Grand Total	795612.636	400989.984	1251491.508	674495.208	601802.652	3724391.988

Exhibit 4-7: The PivotTable after Step 2 of the Independent Practice Activity

3	Sum of Sales		Quarter ▼				
4	Year ▼	Product ▼	Qtr1	Qtr2	Qtr3	Qtr4	Grand Total
5	2001	Anise Seeds	26000	33112	28874	27220	115206
6		Basil Leaf	13800	15080	12821	16363	58064
7		Cassia	45000	43983	46343	45892	181218
8		Chives	18300	25034	28679	25655	97668
9		Cloves	20343	24000	23034	19765	87142
10	2001 Total		123443	141209	139751	134895	539298
11	2002	Anise Seeds	29380	37416.56	32627.62	30758.6	130182.78
12		Basil Leaf	15594	17040.4	14487.73	18490.19	65612.32
13		Cassia	50850	49700.79	52367.59	51857.96	204776.34
14		Chives	20679	28288.42	32407.27	28990.15	110364.84
15		Cloves	22987.59	27120	26028.42	22334.45	98470.46
16	2002 Total		139490.59	159566.17	157918.63	152431.35	609406.74

Exhibit 4-8: The PivotTable after Step3 of the Independent Practice Activity

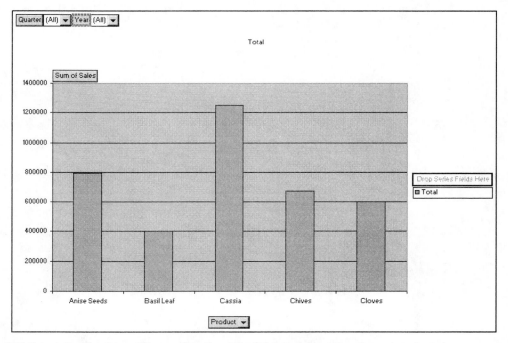

Exhibit 4-9: The PivotChart after Step 6 of the Independent Practice Activity

Review questions

1 What is a PivotTable?

2 What menu choice would you use to begin the creation of a PivotTable?

3 Can you directly change the data in a PivotTable? If not, how do you change the data?

4 Why would you use a PivotChart?

5 How do you create a PivotChart?

Unit 5

Exporting and importing

Unit time: 60 minutes

Complete this unit, and you'll know how to:

A Export data from Excel to a text file, and import data from a text file into an Excel workbook.

B Import XML data into a workbook, and export data from a workbook to an XML data file.

C Use Microsoft Query and the Web query feature to import data from external databases.

Topic A: Exporting and importing text files

This topic covers the following Microsoft Office Specialist exam objective.

#	Objective
XL03S-5-10	Converting files to different file formats for transportability (e.g., .csv, .txt)

Data sharing options

Explanation

You can share information between Excel and other programs in a number of ways, including by using linked objects and copied data. Another way to share data is to export it from Excel to another format or to import data from another format into Excel. Excel can import from and export to several formats, including text files.

Use the Save As command to export data

You can use the Save As command to save an Excel workbook in a file format associated with the program in which you want to use the data. However, an Excel workbook that's saved in a different file format might not retain its original formatting.

When you save an Excel workbook in the Text (Tab delimited) file format, the text and values in the cells are saved as they appear in the Excel worksheet. If the cells contain formulas instead of values, however, the formulas are saved as text.

In a text file, tab characters separate the columns of data, and each row of data starts in a new paragraph. In addition, the formatting, graphics, and objects are not saved when you export data to a text file.

Do it!   **A-1:   Exporting Excel data to a text file**

Here's how	Here's why
1 Open Exporting	From the current unit folder.
2 Choose **File**, **Save As...**	To open the Save As dialog box. The default name of the file is Exporting.
From the Save as type list, select **Text (Tab delimited)**	This will save the worksheet as a tab-delimited text file.
Click **Save**	To save the worksheet as a text file. A Microsoft Excel dialog box appears, stating that Excel will not save those features that are not compatible with the Text (Tab delimited) file format.
Click **Yes**	To keep the tab-delimited format.
3 Click **Start**	
Choose **Programs**, **Accessories**, **Notepad**	To open the Notepad program.
Open the Exporting text file	(From the current unit folder.) The data from the Exporting worksheet appears in the text file. All the sales figures that contain commas appear in double quotation marks.
Close Notepad	
4 Switch to Excel	If necessary.
5 Close the workbook	You don't need to save changes.

Import data

Explanation

You can open a file created in a program other than Excel by using the Open command in Excel. After importing the data, you can save the file either in its original format or as an Excel workbook.

To import a file into an Excel workbook, choose File, Open. In the Open dialog box, specify the type of file you want to import, select the file, and click Open.

If you're importing a text file, Excel displays the Text Import Wizard, guiding you through the process of converting the text data into an Excel worksheet. You can also separate text into columns (after importing) by choosing Data, Text to Columns.

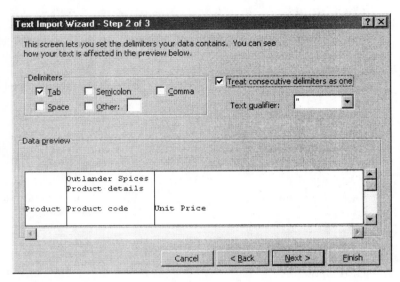

Exhibit 5-1: Step 2 of the Text Import Wizard

Do it!

A-2: Importing data from a text file into a workbook

Here's how	Here's why
1 Open Notepad	Choose Start, Programs, Accessories, Notepad.
Open the Product text file	You'll import data from this text file into Excel. This file contains details for ten products. The data in this file is separated by tab spaces.
Close Notepad	
2 Switch to Excel	If necessary.
3 Choose **File, Open...**	
From the Look in list, select the current unit folder	If necessary.
From the Files of type list, select **Text Files**	To display all the text files in the current unit folder.
Select **Product**	To select the file you want to import.

4	Click **Open**	To open Step 1 of the Text Import Wizard. Under Original data type, Delimited is selected. The Start import at row box displays 1.
	Click **Next**	Step 2 of the Text Import Wizard helps you set the delimiter and shows you a preview of the data. Here, Tab is the default delimiter.
	Under Data preview, observe the box	This box shows you how the data will look in Excel. A few blank columns appear because of the consecutive tab spaces.
	Check **Treat consecutive delimiters as one**	To remove the blank columns, as shown in Exhibit 5-1.
5	Click **Next**	In Step 3 of the Text Import Wizard, you can specify the data format for each column.
6	Click **Finish**	

	A	B	C
		Outlander Spices	
		Product details	
	Product	Product co	Unit Price
	Cassia	P001	$3.25
	Catnip Lea	P002	$2.75
	Celery See	P003	$1.75
	Basil Leaf	P004	$3.00
	Chamomile	P005	$2.25
	Chili Pepp	P006	$2.25
	Chinese S	P007	$2.75
	Cinnamon	P008	$3.00
	Chives	P009	$2.50
	Cilantro Fl	P010	$1.75

To close the Text Import Wizard. The worksheet shows the data from the Product text file in an Excel workbook.

7	Choose **File, Save As...**	To open the Save As dialog box. The File name box displays Product, and the Save as type list displays Text (Tab delimited).
	From the Save as type list, select **Microsoft Office Excel Workbook**	(You might have to scroll up the list to view the option.) To save the data in an Excel worksheet.
	Edit the File name box to read **My product**	
	Click **Save**	
8	Close the workbook	

Topic B: Exporting and importing XML data

This topic covers the following Microsoft Office Specialist exam objectives.

#	Objective
XL03E-1-15	Structure workbooks using XML
	• Adding, modifying and deleting maps
	• Managing elements and attributes in XML workbooks (e.g., adding, modifying, deleting, cutting, copying)
	• Defining XML options (e.g., applying XML view options)
XL03E-4-2	Exporting structured data from Excel

What is XML?

Explanation

Extensible Markup Language (XML) is a set of rules for structuring and designing data formats that are exchanged between applications. You can import data from an XML file into an Excel workbook. You can also export data from a workbook to an XML file. To import or export XML data, you use the XML Source task pane to map the workbook to a user-defined XML schema (.xsd file).

The XML Source task pane

The XML Source task pane helps you map an Excel workbook to an XML schema. This task pane also provides options for importing and exporting XML data. You can also refresh the imported data to reflect the latest changes in the source.

To map a workbook to a user-defined XML schema:

1 Choose Data, XML, XML Source to display the XML Source task pane, and choose View, Toolbars, List to display the List toolbar as shown in Exhibit 5-2.

2 In the task pane, click XML Maps to open the XML Maps dialog box, as shown in Exhibit 5-3.

3 Click Add to open the Select XML Source dialog box. Browse to locate the .xsd file, and click Open.

4 In the Multiple Roots dialog box that appears, select the .xsd file, and click OK.

5 Click OK to close the XML Maps dialog box. The file and the elements in it appear in the XML Source task pane.

6 To map the XML schema to the workbook, drag the elements from the task pane to the corresponding cells in the workbook. The mapped areas appear in blue with nonprintable borders.

Defining XML options

The XML Source task pane also provides options to display XML data in a worksheet in different formats. To choose an option, click the Options button in the XML Source task pane, and select the option you want. The options are:

- **Preview Data in Task Pane** — Displays data in the XML Source task pane when you import XML data.

- **Hide Help Text in the Task Pane** — Hides the help text that appears below the list of schema elements in the XML Source task pane.

- **Automatically Merge Elements When Mapping** — Expands an XML List automatically when you drag an element from the XML Source task pane to a cell that is outside the XML List but adjacent to it.

- **My Data Has Headings** — Uses existing data as column headings when you create XML maps.

- **Hide Border of Inactive Lists** — Hides the border of a mapped cell or XML List when you deselect the cell or XML List.

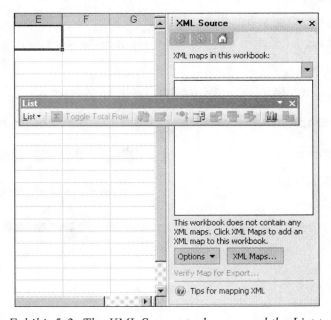

Exhibit 5-2: The XML Source task pane and the List toolbar

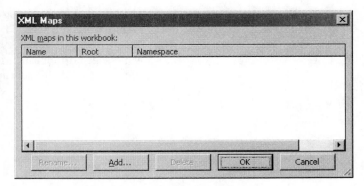

Exhibit 5-3: The XML Maps dialog box

Do it!

B-1: Using the XML Source task pane

Here's how	Here's why
1 Open Employees	(You might need to select Microsoft Office Excel Workbook from the Files of type list in the Open dialog box.) You'll create an XML map for this workbook.
2 Save the workbook as **My employees**	In the current unit folder.
3 Choose **Data**, **XML**, **XML Source...**	To display the XML Source task pane.
Choose **View**, **Toolbars**, **List**	To display the List toolbar, as shown in Exhibit 5-2.
4 Click **XML Maps**	(In the XML Source task pane.) To open the XML Maps dialog box, as shown in Exhibit 5-3.
Click **Add**	To open the Select XML Source dialog box.
From the Look in list, select the current unit folder	If necessary.
Select **EmployeeRecord**	This is the file containing the XML schema.
Click **Open**	

Multiple Roots

The selected XML schema contains more than one root node. Microsoft Excel can only create an XML map based on one of the root nodes.

Please select a root:

EmployeeRecord
MyEmployeeRecord

[OK] [Cancel]

	The Multiple Roots dialog box opens with EmployeeRecord selected.
Click **OK**	A message box appears, asking if you want to continue adding this schema to your workbook.
Click **Yes**	

5   Click **OK**

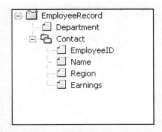

To close the XML Maps dialog box. You can see the .xsd file along with its elements in the XML Source task pane.

6   Drag **Department** from the XML Source task pane as shown

To map the element Department in the XML schema to the worksheet.

Deselect A8

(Click anywhere in the worksheet.) Now, the cell has a blue border, indicating that the cell is mapped to an XML schema.

7   Drag **EmployeeID** to A11

Drag **Name** to B11

Drag **Region** to C11

Drag **Earnings** to D11

8   Select E11

To deselect the mapped cells. You'll hide the border of mapped cells that are deselected.

9   Click as shown

In the XML Source task pane.

Select **Hide Border of Inactive Lists**

To hide the border around mapped cells. The blue border is no longer visible.

10 Select D11

A border appears around the list.

11 Click as shown

In the XML Source task pane.

Select **Hide Border of Inactive Lists**

To show the border of mapped cells that are deselected. Notice the blue border on cell A8.

12 Update the workbook

Import XML data into a workbook

Explanation
You can import data in an XML format into a workbook after creating an XML map. To import XML data:

1 Choose Data, XML, Import to open the Import XML dialog box. You can also use the Import button on the List toolbar.
2 Select the XML file containing the data. You can use the Look in list to locate the file, if necessary.
3 Click Import. The values in the XML file appear in the corresponding cells in the workbook, as shown in Exhibit 5-4.

Department			
Human resources			
EmployeeID ▼	Name ▼	Region ▼	Earnings ▼
E001	Malcolm Pingault	East ⟨!⟩	$73,500
E006	Annie Philips	West	$60,000
E011	Paul Anderson	East	$180,000
E019	Jamie Morrison	East	$62,000
✱			

Exhibit 5-4: The worksheet after Step 3

Do it!
B-2: Importing XML data into a workbook

Here's how	Here's why
1 Choose **Data**, **XML**, **Import...**	To open the Import XML dialog box.
2 Select **EmployeeInfo**	(From the current unit folder.) This file contains values for fields such as Department, EmployeeID, Name, Region, and Earnings in the workbook.
3 Click **Import**	You'll see that the values corresponding to Department, EmployeeID, Name, Region, and Earnings appear in the corresponding cells, as shown in Exhibit 5-4. The Trace Error button appears because Earnings values are stored as text instead of numbers.
4 Update and close the workbook	

Export data from workbooks to XML data files

Explanation
You can modify the data in a workbook and then export it in an XML format so that it can be used by other applications. You can add or delete records in the workbook.

For you to export data, the workbook should contain a valid XML map. Excel will validate the worksheet data against this map before exporting it.

To export the workbook data, you can choose Data, XML, Export, or use the Export button on the List toolbar.

Do it!

B-3:   Exporting data from a workbook to an XML data file

Here's how	Here's why
1 Open Export as XML	From the current unit folder.
2 Display the XML Source task pane	(If necessary. To do so, choose Data, XML, XML Source.) The workbook is mapped to EmployeeRecord.
3 Save the workbook as **My export as XML**	In the current unit folder.
4 In A21, enter **E038**	To enter the employee ID for someone who has joined the Accounting department.
In B21, enter **David Ford**	
5 Select C11	You'll copy the data in this cell to C21.
Click	The Copy button is on the Standard toolbar.
Select C21	
Click	The Paste button is on the Standard toolbar.
6 Copy D17 to D21	
7 Select A16:D16	This is the record for an employee who has left the Accounting department.
Choose **Edit**, **Delete Row**	To delete the record.
8 Update the workbook	
9 Choose **Data**, **XML**, **Export...**	To open the Export XML dialog box.
From the Save in list, select the current unit folder	If necessary.
In the File name box, type **My export as XML**	
10 Click **Export**	To export the workbook as an XML file.

Delete XML maps

Explanation

After importing or exporting data, you no longer need to map the workbook to an XML schema. Therefore, you can delete the XML maps. When you delete a map, the data in the workbook remains.

To delete an XML map:

1   In the XML Source task pane, click XML Maps to open the XML Maps dialog box.

2   Select the XML map you want to delete.

3   Click Delete. A message box appears, warning that you'll no longer be able to import or export XML data by using the XML map. Click OK.

4   Click OK.

Do it!

B-4:   Deleting an XML map

Here's how	Here's why
1 Click **XML Maps...**	(You might need to scroll to the bottom of the XML Source task pane.) To open the XML Maps dialog box.
2 In the XML maps in this workbook list, select the XML map	
Click **Delete**	A message box appears, warning you that you'll no longer be able to import or export XML data using this XML map.
Click **OK**	(To delete the XML map and close the message box.) The XML Maps dialog box no longer displays the XML map.
3 Click **OK**	To close the XML Maps dialog box.
4 Observe the workbook	The data in the workbook remains intact.
5 Close the workbook	

Topic C: Querying external databases

This topic covers the following Microsoft Office Specialist exam objectives.

#	Objective
XL03E-4-1	Bringing information into Excel from external sources
XL03E-4-1	Linking to Web page data

Microsoft Query

Explanation

Microsoft Query helps you retrieve data that meets certain conditions in one or more tables of a database. For example, from an Employee table, you can retrieve the records of all people who work in the Marketing department. To retrieve data by using Microsoft Query:

1   Choose Data, Import External Data, New Database Query to start the Microsoft Query program and to open the Choose Data Source dialog box.

2   On the Databases tab, select <New Data Source> and click OK to open the Create New Data Source dialog box. Specify the name of the data source and select a driver for the database. Click Connect to open the ODBC Microsoft Access Setup dialog box.

3   Under Database, click Select to open the Select Database dialog box. Select the source database, and then return to the Choose Data Source dialog box.

4   Select the data source, and click OK to open the Choose Columns dialog box of the Query Wizard. Add the tables and fields you want to include in your result set. Click Next to open the Filter Data dialog box of the Query Wizard.

5   Specify the conditions you want the data to meet. Click Next to open the Sort Order dialog box of the Query Wizard.

6   Specify the sort order for the data. Click Next to open the Finish dialog box of the Query Wizard.

7   Select Return Data to Microsoft Excel. Click Finish to open the Import Data dialog box.

8   Specify whether you want to place the data in the existing worksheet or in a new worksheet.

9   Click OK to import the data.

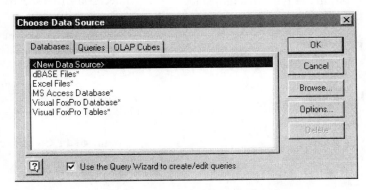

Exhibit 5-5: The Choose Data Source dialog box

Do it!

C-1: Using Microsoft Query to get data from an external database

Here's how	Here's why
1 Open Querying databases	(You might need to select Microsoft Excel Files from the Files of type list in the Open dialog box.) This workbook contains two worksheets. QueryDb is the active sheet. You'll use the Microsoft Query program to retrieve data from an Access database and place it in this worksheet.
2 Save the workbook as **My querying databases**	In the current unit folder.
3 Choose **Data**, **Import External Data**, **New Database Query...**	To open the Choose Data Source dialog box, as shown in Exhibit 5-5. By default, the Databases tab is active. You can either select an existing data source or create a new one. The taskbar button for Microsoft Query appears.
4 Click **OK**	To open the Create New Data Source dialog box.
In the first box, type **Employee**	To specify the name of the new data source.
Select as shown	

Select a driver for the type of database you want to access:

2.

Driver da Microsoft para arquivos texto (*.txt; *.csv)
Driver do Microsoft Access (*.mdb)
3. Driver do Microsoft dBase (*.dbf)
Driver do Microsoft Excel(*.xls)
Driver do Microsoft Paradox (*.db)
Driver para o Microsoft Visual FoxPro
4. Microsoft Access Driver (*.mdb)
Microsoft Access-Treiber (*.mdb)
Microsoft dBase Driver (*.dbf)

	To specify the database driver.
5 Click **Connect**	To open the ODBC Microsoft Access Setup dialog box.
Under Database, click **Select**	To open the Select Database dialog box.
From the Directories list, select the current unit folder	(If necessary.) To specify the folder that contains the database.
From the Database Name list, select **Employee.mdb**	To specify the database from which you'll import data.
6 Click **OK**	To return to the ODBC Microsoft Access Setup dialog box.
Click **OK**	To return to the Create New Data Source dialog box.

7 From the last list, select **Employees**	To specify the default table for building queries.
Click **OK**	To return to the Choose Data Source dialog box. The Employee data source has been added to the list and is selected.
8 Click **OK**	To close the Choose Data Source dialog box and open the Choose Columns dialog box of the Query Wizard. In the Available tables and columns list, Employees is selected.
Click [>]	To include all the columns of the Employees table in the query. The columns of the Employees table now appear in the Columns in your query list.
9 Click **Next**	To open the Filter Data dialog box of the Query Wizard. The group box under "Only include rows where" is not available and has no name.
From the Column to filter list, select **Dept code**	
	The group box under "Only include rows where" is now available and is named "Dept code." The first list under Dept code is also available.
From the first list, select **equals**	To specify the comparison operator for the query.
From the second list, select **MKTG**	This specifies that the result of this query will include only those rows where the Dept code is MKTG.
10 Click **Next**	To open the Sort Order dialog box of the Query Wizard.
From the Sort by list, select **Region**	This will sort data by Region. By default, Ascending is selected.
11 Click **Next**	To open the Finish dialog box of the Query Wizard. By default, Return Data to Microsoft Excel is selected.
12 Click **Finish**	The Import Data dialog box appears, prompting you to specify the destination location for the data. Existing worksheet is selected by default.
13 Click **OK**	The records of all employees in the Marketing department appear in the worksheet. The External Data toolbar also appears.
14 Update the workbook	

The Web query feature

Explanation

If you want to analyze data on the Web, such as online currency rates or stock quotes, you can create a Web query.

When you run a Web query, Excel retrieves data that has been formatted with Hypertext Markup Language (HTML) or Extensible Markup Language (XML).

HTML and XML

The focus of HTML, which consists primarily of predefined tags, is the appearance of the content in a browser window. XML, on the other hand, focuses on the content and not on its appearance. There are no predefined tags in XML; instead, you create your own tags to give your data meaning and structure. Both markup languages are related to a parent language, SGML (Standard Generalized Markup Language), which provides rules for marking up documents and data.

Do it!

C-2: Discussing the Web query feature

Questions and answers

1 Which Excel feature do you use to analyze stock market quotes on the Web?

2 What are the file formats in which a Web query retrieves data?

3 What are the main differences between HTML and XML?

Use the Web query feature to retrieve data from the Web

Explanation

To retrieve data from a Web page:

1   Choose Data, Import External Data, New Web Query to open the New Web Query dialog box.

2   In the Address box, specify the address of the Web page from which you want to retrieve data, as shown in Exhibit 5-6.

3   Click the arrow next to the tables you want to select.

4   Click Options to open the Web Query Options dialog box.

5   Select the format in which you want the data to be displayed. Click OK.

6   Click Import. The Import Data dialog box appears. Specify whether you want to get data in an existing worksheet or a new worksheet. Click OK.

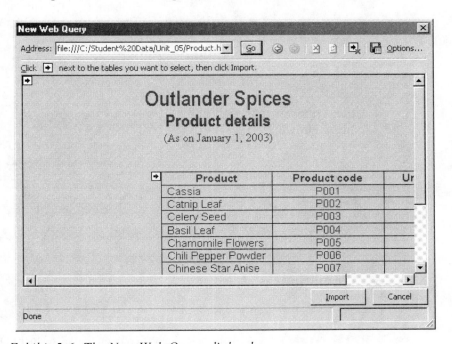

Exhibit 5-6: The New Web Query dialog box

Do it!

C-3:   Using Web query to get data from the Web

Here's how	Here's why
1 Activate the WebQ sheet	You'll use the Web query program to retrieve data from a Web page.
2 Choose **Data**, **Import External Data**, **New Web Query...**	To open the New Web Query dialog box.
3 In the Address box, type **C:\Student Data\Unit_<##>\Product.htm**	(Substitute <##> with the current unit number.) This is the address of the Web page that contains the relevant data.
Click **Go**	The preview of the Web page appears in the dialog box.
4 Click the arrow to the left of the table as shown	(As on January 1, 2003) **Product** Click to select this table. Catnip Leaf
	To import data from only the table on the Web page.
5 Click **Options** as shown	Options...
	To open the Web Query Options dialog box.
Under Formatting, select **Full HTML formatting**	To retain the current formatting of the table.
Click **OK**	
6 Click **Import**	The Import Data dialog box appears. By default, the Existing worksheet option is selected.
Click **OK**	The data from the table on the Web page appears in the worksheet. The External Data toolbar also appears.
7 Update and close the workbook	

Unit summary: Exporting and importing

Topic A In this topic, you learned how to **export data** from Excel to a text file. You learned how to **import data** from a text file into an Excel workbook. You also learned that you can separate the imported data into columns.

Topic B In this topic, you learned how to use the **XML Source task pane** to create an **XML map** for a workbook. You also learned how to use the XML Source task pane to **import XML data** into an Excel workbook and to **export data** from a workbook to an XML file. In addition, you learned how to **delete** XML maps.

Topic C In this topic, you learned how to use **Microsoft Query** to retrieve data from an Access database. You also learned how to use the **Web query** feature to retrieve data from Web pages in HTML or XML format.

Independent practice activity

1 Open Exporting practice. (Ensure that Export is the active worksheet.)

2 Save the workbook as **My query practice**.

3 Export data from the Export worksheet to a text file. Save the text file as **My exporting practice**.

4 Open the exported file in Notepad. Because some product names are longer or shorter than others, the tabbed columns might not appear neatly on your screen. Close Notepad.

5 Activate the XML worksheet. Create a workbook map by using EmployeeRecord, and link the elements in the file to the corresponding fields in the workbook. (*Hint:* In the XML Source task pane, click XML Maps.)

6 Export the data in the XML worksheet as an XML file. Save the XML file as **My XML practice**.

7 Activate the My exporting practice worksheet. By using Microsoft Query, import the Sales employees table from the Employee.mdb database into a new Excel worksheet. Ensure that the imported data is sorted in ascending order by the values in the field Lname. Compare your results with Exhibit 5-7.

8 Update the workbook. (*Hint:* If necessary, from the Save as type list, select Microsoft Excel Workbook.)

9 Close the XML Source task pane, the List toolbar, and the External Data toolbar.

10 Close the workbook.

	A	B	C	D
1	Ecode	Lname	Fname	Region
2	E-02	Lee	Shannon	South
3	E-03	McGregor	Melinda	West
4	E-04	Overmire	James	North
5	E-01	Pingault	Malcolm	East

Exhibit 5-7: The data imported in Step 6 of Independent Practice Activity

Review questions

1 An Excel workbook that's saved in a different file format will retain its original formatting. True or False.

2 List three ways that the XML Source task pane is useful.

3 List two ways you can export a workbook to an XML file.

4 List the steps you would use to delete an XML map.

5 What is Microsoft Query?

Unit 6

Using analytical options

Unit time: 50 minutes

Complete this unit, and you'll know how to:

A Use the Goal Seek and Solver utilities to meet a target output for a formula by adjusting the values in the input cells.

B Install and use the Analysis ToolPak.

C Create scenarios to save various sets of input values that produce different results.

D Create views to save different sets of worksheet display and print settings.

Topic A: Working with Goal Seek and Solver

This topic covers the following Microsoft Office Specialist exam objectives.

#	Objective
XL03E-1-7	Performing What-If analysis
XL03E-1-7	Using the Solver add-in

What-if analysis

Explanation

You might want a formula to return a specific result, but you might not know the input values that will provide that result. For example, you might want to take out a loan for which the maximum monthly payment you can afford is $500. Based on this, you might want to know a possible combination of period, interest rate, and principal amount. In this case, you can use Goal Seek and Solver to find the input values.

The Goal Seek and Solver utilities are used to perform *what-if analysis*. This type of analysis involves changing the values in a worksheet and observing how these changes affect the results of the formulas. You use Goal Seek to solve problems that have one variable. Solver helps you analyze problems that have multiple variables and constraints.

The Goal Seek utility

Use the Goal Seek utility to solve a formula based on the value that you want the formula to return. To use the Goal Seek utility:

1   Choose Tools, Goal Seek to open the Goal Seek dialog box.
2   In the Set cell box, specify the cell that contains the formula you want to solve.
3   In the To value box, enter the result you want.
4   In the By changing cell box, specify the cell that contains the value you want to adjust.
5   Click OK.

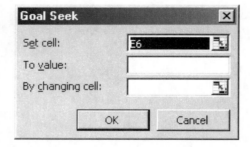

Exhibit 6-1: The Goal Seek dialog box

Do it!   **A-1:   Using Goal Seek to solve for a single variable**

Here's how	Here's why
1 Open Analytical options	(From the current unit folder.) This workbook contains four worksheets. Goal seeking is the active sheet.
2 Save the workbook as **My analytical options**	In the current unit folder.
3 Select E6	This cell displays a monthly payment of -$3,417.76 for a loan amount of $100,000. You'll use Goal Seek to calculate the loan amount that you can obtain if you can afford a monthly payment of $10,000, given a period of 36 months and an interest rate of 14%.
Observe the Formula bar	*fx* =PMT(D6%/12,C6,B6) The PMT function calculates the monthly payment for the loan amount in B6 based on the annual interest rate in D6 and the repayment period in C6.
4 Choose **Tools**, **Goal Seek...**	(To open the Goal Seek dialog box, as shown in Exhibit 6-1.) The Set cell box displays E6. This cell contains the formula you want to solve.
In the To value box, type **−10000**	This is the result you want the formula in E6 to return.
In the By changing cell box, type **B6**	This is the cell containing the loan amount, the value that will be adjusted.
5 Click **OK**	 The Goal Seek Status dialog box tells you that Goal Seek has found a solution, which you can choose to accept or reject. The target value represents the value you asked the formula to return. The current value represents the solution found by Goal Seek.
Click **OK**	With a monthly payment of $10,000, for a given period of 36 months and an interest rate of 14%, you can afford a loan of $292,589.

6 Find the loan amount that the company can obtain from the NewCiti bank if it pays $15,000 per month for 42 months

(Use Goal Seek.) You'll get $487,820 as the loan amount.

7 Update the workbook

The Solver utility

Explanation

You use the Solver utility to perform complex what-if analysis. Solver helps you determine optimal values for a cell by adjusting multiple cells used in a formula. You can also apply multiple constraints on one or more cells used in a formula.

To use the Solver utility:

1 Choose Tools, Solver to open the Solver Parameters dialog box.

2 In the Set Target Cell box, specify the cell that contains the formula you want to solve.

3 Under Equal To, select the appropriate option—Max, Min, or Value of—for the result of the target cell.

4 In the By Changing Cells box, specify the cells in which the values will be adjusted.

5 In the Subject to the Constraints box, add any constraints you want by using the Add button. For example, if you were changing a cell that contained a period of months, you would want to constrain that cell to contain whole numbers.

6 Click Solve.

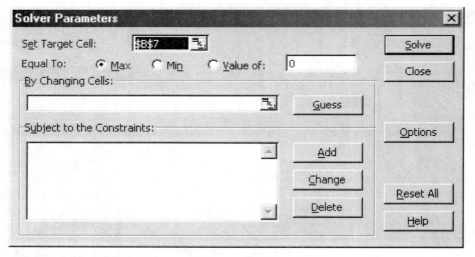

Exhibit 6-2: The Solver Parameters dialog box

Do it!   **A-2:   Using Solver to solve for multiple variables**

Here's how	Here's why
1 Activate the Solver sheet	You'll use the Solver utility to attain a total profit of 35% by adjusting the values of Total sales, Cost of sales, Overhead, and Marketing.
2 Select F15	You'll use Solver to figure out the input values that result in 35% projected total profit, given certain constraints.
3 Choose **Tools**, **Solver...**	(You might need to click the down chevron.) To open the Solver Parameters dialog box, as shown in Exhibit 6-2.
In the Set Target Cell box, select **F15**	To specify the target cell.
In the Equal To area, select **Value of**	To specify the precise value you want the target cell to attain.
Edit the box next to the Value of option to read **35**	This is the value you want the target cell to attain.
4 In the By Changing Cells box, enter **B7:E8, B11:E12**	These are the cells in which the values will be adjusted. They represent various costs and sales revenue.
5 Under Subject to the Constraints, click **Add**	

To open the Add Constraint dialog box. You'll specify the constraints here.

6 In the Cell Reference box, select **B12**	You'll apply a constraint to this cell, specifying that the company cannot spend more than $10,000 on marketing in quarter 1.
In the list, verify that <= is selected	This is the less-than-or-equal-to operator.
In the Constraint box, type **10000**	This value and the selected operator specify that B12 must have a value less than or equal to $10,000.
Click **Add**	To add the constraint to the Subject to the Constraints list. The boxes in the Add Constraint dialog box are refreshed, and the insertion point is in the Cell Reference box.

7	Select F9	(You might need to move the Add Constraint dialog box.) You'll specify the second constraint on this cell. The constraint is that the gross profit for the company cannot be less than $150,000.
	From the list, select **>=**	This is the greater-than-or-equal-to operator.
	In the Constraint box, type **150000**	This value and the selected operator specify that F9 must have a value greater than or equal to $150,000.
	Click **OK**	To add this second constraint to the Subject to the Constraints list and return to the Solver Parameters dialog box.
8	Click **Solve**	To trigger Solver to adjust the values. After a moment, the Solver Results dialog box appears. Verify that Keep Solver Solution is selected. This ensures that the solution found by the Solver is retained.
	Click **OK**	The adjusted values appear in the worksheet. F15 displays the Profit % as 35. The value in B12 shows the Marketing expenses in quarter 1 as less than $10,000 and the value in F9 shows the Gross profit as greater than $150,000.
9	Update the workbook	

Topic B: Working with the Analysis ToolPak

This topic covers the following Microsoft Office Specialist exam objective.

#	Objective
XL03E-1-7	Projecting values using analysis tools (e.g., Analysis ToolPak)

Analysis ToolPak overview

Explanation

The Analysis ToolPak is a set of analysis tools, including Correlation, Covariance, Regression, and Sampling. Each tool consists of macro functions needed to perform the corresponding analysis.

Although the Analysis ToolPak is a component of Excel software, it isn't automatically installed. Therefore, to use the analysis tools, you must first install the Analysis ToolPak. The following table lists the tools available in the ToolPak:

Analysis Tools	Description
Anova	Performs variance analysis.
Correlation	Examines the relationship between two sets of data. Each set of data can have different units of measurement.
Covariance	Examines the relationship between two data ranges.
Descriptive Statistics	Summarizes information related to different types of data used in an analysis.
Exponential Smoothing	Adjusts the output based on previous forecasts.
F-Test Two Sample for Variances	Compares two population variances.
Fourier Analysis	Solves linear equations and analyzes periodic data by using the Fast Fourier Transform method.
Histogram	Determines the frequency in a data range.
Moving Average	Forecasts values for a period based on the average of previous forecasts.
Random Number Generation	Generates random numbers based on several distributions to fill a range.
Rank and Percentile	Calculates the rank and percentile of each value in a data set.
Regression	Performs linear regression analysis to determine the relation between different values.
Sampling	Creates samples from a population.
t-Test	Tests the means of various populations.
z-Test	Tests the means of known variances.

To install the Analysis ToolPak:

1   Choose Tools, Add-Ins to open the Add-Ins dialog box.

2   In the Add-Ins available list, check Analysis ToolPak.

3   Click OK.

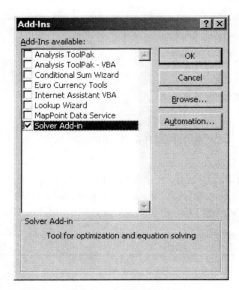

Exhibit 6-3: The Add-Ins dialog box

Do it!

B-1:   Installing the Analysis ToolPak

Here's how	Here's why
1 Activate the Sampling sheet	
2 Choose **Tools**, **Add-Ins...**	To open the Add-Ins dialog box, as shown in Exhibit 6-3.
3 In the Add-Ins available list, check **Analysis ToolPak**	
Click **OK**	To close the Add-Ins dialog box and to install the Analysis ToolPak.
	If a message box appears asking if you'd like to install this add-in now, click Yes. You might need to insert the Microsoft Office 2003 installation disk.
4 Choose **Tools**, **Data Analysis...**	To open the Data Analysis dialog box. The Data Analysis option was added to the Tools menu when you installed the Analysis ToolPak.
Observe the Analysis Tools list	The list displays the data analysis tools available in the ToolPak.
5 Click **Cancel**	To close the dialog box.

Use analysis tools

Explanation

After installing the Analysis ToolPak, you can select any tool from the Analysis Tools list. For example, you might want to create a sampling distribution for the sales in a specific region for a specific year. To perform this analysis, you have to select samples from the sales report. You can use the Sampling analysis tool to get these samples from a data range. You can select data samples either in a random manner or at regular intervals.

To select sample data by using the Sampling analysis tool:

1 Choose Tools, Data Analysis to open the Data Analysis dialog box.
2 From the Analysis Tools list, select Sampling.
3 Click OK to open the Sampling dialog box.
4 In the Input Range box, select the range of data from which you want to select samples.
5 Specify a sampling method and an output option.
6 Click OK.

Do it!

B-2:   Using the Sampling analysis tool

Here's how	Here's why
1 Observe the sales data in column D	This column contains sales figures for the East region that range from $15,345 to $44,353.
Choose **Tools, Data Analysis...**	To open the Data Analysis dialog box.
2 From the Analysis Tools list, select **Sampling**	You'll select data samples that represent sales in the East region.
Click **OK**	To open the Sampling dialog box.
3 In the Input Range box, select **D5:D24**	To specify the range of data from which samples are to be selected.
4 Under Sampling Method, select **Periodic**	You'll select samples at regular intervals.
In the Period box, type **5**	You'll select a sample at every fifth instance of data in the range.
5 Under Output options, select **Output Range**	You'll specify the range where the samples should appear. You can also display the output in a new worksheet or a new workbook.
In the Output Range box, select **E5:E8**	
6 Click **OK**	Data samples appear in E5:E8. They are representative of the sales for the East region.
7 Update the workbook	

Topic C: Working with scenarios

This topic covers the following Microsoft Office Specialist exam objective.

#	Objective
XL03E-1-6	Managing scenarios

What's a scenario?

Explanation

Scenarios are sets of input values that produce different results. For example, in a budget projection worksheet, you could have one scenario that includes conservative sales figures and another scenario representing more aggressive sales. Instead of creating new scenarios every time, you can modify existing scenarios. In a worksheet containing multiple scenarios, you can switch among them to view the results for different input values. In addition, you can merge scenarios from other worksheets.

Create a scenario

You can use the Scenario Manager dialog box to create a scenario:

1 Choose Tools, Scenarios to open the Scenario Manager dialog box.
2 Click the Add button to open the Add Scenario dialog box.
3 In the Scenario name box, specify the name of the scenario.
4 In the Changing cells box, specify the cells that contain the values you want to change.
5 Click OK to open the Scenario Values dialog box.
6 In the Scenario Values dialog box, specify values for the changing cells.
7 Click OK to create the scenario.

After creating the scenario, you can modify it by editing values for the changing cells. To edit values:

1 In the Scenario Manager dialog box, select the scenario that you want to change.
2 Click Edit to open the Edit Scenario dialog box.
3 Click OK.
4 In the Scenario Values dialog box, specify values for the changing cells.
5 Click OK to modify the scenario.

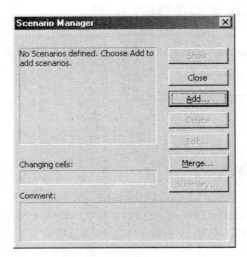

Exhibit 6-4: The Scenario Manager dialog box

Do it!

C-1: Creating scenarios

Here's how	Here's why
1 Activate the Scenarios sheet	You'll create scenarios for this worksheet to see how different Cost of sales values will affect the Gross profit, Net profit, and Profit %.
2 Select B8:E8	
Choose **Tools, Scenarios...**	To open the Scenario Manager dialog box, as shown in Exhibit 6-4. A message is displayed, stating that no scenarios have been defined.
Click **Add**	To open the Add Scenario dialog box.
3 In the Scenario name box, type **Original profit**	This is the name of the scenario that will preserve the original values. The Changing cells box displays the references of the selected cells.
Edit the Comment box to read **Original projected profit**	This comment describes the scenario.
Click **OK**	

B8	25000
C8	42050
D8	59450
E8	60450

To open the Scenario Values dialog box. All the boxes display the current values of the respective cells.

4 Click **Add**

To add the scenario Original profit to the Scenarios list and return to the Add Scenario dialog box. This scenario will preserve the original values in changing cells.

5 In the Scenario name box, type **Decreased cost of sales**

This is the name of the scenario you are about to create.

Edit the Comment box to read **Projected profit with decreased cost of sales**

This comment describes the new scenario.

Click **OK**

To open the Scenario Values dialog box.

6 Type the values as shown

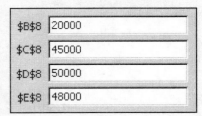

B8	23000
C8	40000
D8	55000
E8	55000

7 Click **OK**

To return to the Scenario Manager dialog box. The Scenarios list displays the names of the two scenarios you just defined.

8 Click **Show**

To apply the Decreased cost of sales scenario. The values in the range B8:E8 change according to the values stored in the Decreased cost of sales scenario. Based on the new Cost of sales values, the values for Gross profit, Net profit, and Profit % also change.

Click **Edit**

To open the Edit Scenario dialog box. The Scenario name box displays Decreased cost of sales.

Click **OK**

To open the Scenario Values dialog box. All the boxes display the current values of the respective cells.

9 Type the values as shown

B8	20000
C8	45000
D8	50000
E8	48000

Click **OK**

To return to the Scenario Manager dialog box.

Click **Close**

10 Update the workbook

Switch among scenarios

You can switch among scenarios to view results based on different input values. To display a scenario, open the Scenario Manager dialog box, select the name of the scenario you want to display, and click the Show button.

The Scenarios list

If you have a worksheet with many scenarios, you can switch among them more easily by adding the Scenario list to a toolbar. To do so, open the Customize dialog box, and display the Tools category on the Commands tab. Find the Scenario list, and drag it to the toolbar where you want it to appear.

Do it!

C-2: Switching among scenarios

Here's how	Here's why
1 Open the Scenario Manager dialog box	(Choose Tools, Scenarios.) In the Scenarios list, Decreased cost of sales is selected by default.
Click **Show**	To apply the changes made to Decreased cost of sales scenario.
2 Click **Close**	The values for Cost of sales values, Gross profit, Net profit, and Profit % have changed.
Observe F15	The Profit % has increased to 33.
3 Choose **Tools, Customize...**	To open the Customize dialog box. You'll add the Scenario list to the Standard toolbar.
Click the **Commands** tab	If necessary.
From the Categories list, select **Tools**	
From the Commands list, drag **Scenario** to the Standard toolbar as shown	
4 Click **Close**	To close the Customize dialog box.
5 Click as shown	
	To display the Scenario list.
Select **Original profit**	You can use this list to switch among scenarios.
6 Open the Customize dialog box	Choose Tools, Customize.
Drag the Scenario list off the Standard toolbar	To remove the Scenario list from the Standard toolbar.
Click **Close**	To close the Customize dialog box.
7 Update the workbook	

Merge scenarios

Explanation

You can merge scenarios from different worksheets so that all scenarios in a source worksheet are copied to the active worksheet. The changing cells in the active worksheet correspond to those in the source worksheet. This ensures that the changes made in the source worksheet are reflected in the active worksheet.

To merge scenarios:

1   Activate the worksheet where you want to merge scenarios.
2   Open the Scenario Manager dialog box.
3   Click Merge.
4   From the Sheet list, select a worksheet that contains the scenarios you want to merge.
5   Click OK to merge scenarios.

The Scenario Summary report

A Scenario Summary report displays the original and current values for the changing cells corresponding to available scenarios. To create a Scenario Summary report:

1   Open the Scenario Manager dialog box.
2   Click Summary to open the Scenario Summary dialog box.
3   In the Result cells box, select the cells that contain the values changed by scenarios.
4   Click OK.

Do it!

C-3:   Merging scenarios from another worksheet

Here's how	Here's why
1 Activate the Solver sheet	You'll merge scenarios to this worksheet from the Scenarios worksheet.
2 Open the Scenario Manager dialog box	(Choose Tools, Scenarios.) There are no scenarios in the Solver worksheet.
3 Click **Merge**	To open the Merge Scenarios dialog box. The Book box displays the name of the workbook from which you'll merge the scenarios. The Sheet list contains the worksheets in the workbook. By default, Goal seeking is selected.
In the Sheet box, select **Scenarios**	You'll merge the scenarios in this worksheet.
4 Click **OK**	To return to the Scenario Manager dialog box. The Scenarios list displays the names of the two scenarios you just merged. By default, Original profit is selected.

5   Select **Decreased cost of sales**

    Click **Show** — To apply the Decreased cost of sales scenario. The values for Cost of sales, Gross profit, Net profit, and Profit % change according to the values stored in the Decreased cost of sales scenario.

    Observe F15 — The Profit % has increased to 36% in the Solver worksheet.

6   Click **Summary**

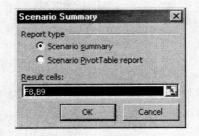

To open the Scenario Summary dialog box. By default, Scenario summary is selected.

    In the Result cells box, select the values as shown

The values in these cells changed when you applied the Decreased cost of sales scenario.

    Click **OK** — To create the Scenario Summary report. You'll see the original and current values in the changing cells and result cells.

7   Update the workbook

Topic D: Working with views

Explanation

Views are different sets of worksheet display and print settings that you can save. For example, in a sales worksheet, you can create a view in which the rows of data for all sales regions except for one are hidden. You can create multiple views for a worksheet and switch among the views to change the display of the worksheet.

Create custom views

To create a view based on current display settings:

1   Choose Views, Custom Views to open the Custom Views dialog box.
2   Click Add to open the Add View dialog box.
3   In the Name box, type a name for the view. Click OK.

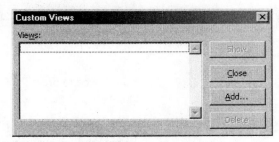

Exhibit 6-5: The Custom Views dialog box

D-1: Creating views

Here's how	Here's why
1 Activate the View sheet	This worksheet contains a sales analysis report.
2 Choose **View**, **Custom Views...**	To open the Custom Views dialog box, as shown in Exhibit 6-5.
Click **Add**	To open the Add View dialog box.
3 In the Name box, type **Original**	

Click **OK**	
4 Select rows 1:3, 5:25, and 47:89	You'll need to press the Ctrl key and then select the rows.
Choose **Format**, **Row**, **Hide**	(You might have to scroll up to view the data.) To hide the selected rows. Now, you can view only the records for the North region.
5 Open the Custom Views dialog box	Choose View, Custom Views.
Click **Add**	To open the Add View dialog box.
6 In the Name box, type **North**	
Click **OK**	
7 Choose **Format**, **Row**, **Unhide**	To display all the rows.
	The rows will not unhide if you have selected anything in the worksheet after hiding the rows in Step 4. In this case, to display the hidden rows, select rows above and below the hidden rows, and choose Format, Row, Unhide.
Create a view named **South** that displays only the records for the South region	Hide all rows except for the rows that display the details for the South region. Then, use the Custom Views dialog box to add the view.
Create a view named **West** that displays only the records for the West region	First, unhide all the hidden rows. Then display only the records for the West region. Finally, use the Custom Views dialog box to add the view.
8 Update the workbook	

Switch among custom views

Explanation

To switch among views, open the Custom Views dialog box. From the Views list, select the view you want to display, and then click the Show button. You can also add the Custom Views list to a toolbar to easily select different views.

Do it!

D-2: Switching among views

Here's how	Here's why
1 Open the Custom Views dialog box	(Choose View, Custom Views.) The Views list displays the names of all available views.
From the Views list, select **Original**	
Click **Show**	To display the records in Original view. Records for all the regions appear in the worksheet.
2 Display North view	Use the Custom Views dialog box.
Display South view	
Display West view	
3 Update and close the workbook	

Unit summary: Using analytical options

Topic A   In this topic, you learned that you use **Goal Seek** to find a specific result for a formula by adjusting the value of one of the input cells. You also learned that you use the **Solver** add-in to determine optimal values for a cell by adjusting multiple cells used in a formula.

Topic B   In this topic, you learned how to install and use the **Analysis ToolPak**. You learned how to use the **Sampling analysis tool** to select samples from a data range.

Topic C   In this topic, you learned how to **create** and **edit scenarios**. You learned that scenarios are used to save sets of input values that produce different results. Then, you learned how to **switch among scenarios** to view different data results in a worksheet. In addition, you learned how to **merge scenarios** and create a **Scenario Summary report**.

Topic D   In this topic, you learned how to create **views**. You learned that views are created to save different sets of worksheet display and print settings. You also learned how to **switch among views** and how doing this changes the display of a worksheet.

Independent practice activity

1 Open Analytical options practice. Goal seeking should be the active worksheet.

2 Save the workbook as **My analytical options practice**.

3 In D6, use Goal Seek to calculate the loan amount for a monthly deduction of $2,300. (*Hint:* Use the Goal Seek dialog box. The loan amount will be $108,250.)

4 Activate the Solver worksheet. Use Solver to calculate a total profit of 30% by adjusting the values for Total sales, Cost of sales, Overhead, and Marketing. When adjusting values, you must ensure that the total overhead for the year cannot be greater than $25,000, and the net profit for the year must be at least $100,000. Compare your results with Exhibit 6-6.

5 Update the workbook.

6 In the Views worksheet, create views named **Accounting**, **Customer support**, **Human resources**, **Marketing**, and **National sales**. Each view should display the details for the respective departments.

7 Add the Custom Views list to the Standard toolbar. Use this list to display each view, and then remove it from the toolbar. (*Hint:* The Custom Views list is in the Views category.)

8 Update and close the workbook.

	Qtr1	Qtr2	Qtr3	Qtr4	Total
Total sales	56202	84402	95702	97452	333758
Cost of sales	38213	40957	58357	59357	196884
Gross profit	17989	43445	37345	38095	136874
Overhead	6407	6427	4527	2427	19788
Marketing	5907	5537	3407	2107	16958
	12314	11964	7934	4534	36747
Net profit	5675	31481	29411	33561	100128
Profit %	10	37	31	34	30

Exhibit 6-6: The Solver worksheet after Step 4 of the Independent Practice Activity

Review questions

1 What utilities can be used to perform what-if analysis?

2 Which utility solves a formula based on the value that you want the formula to return?

3 List the steps you would use to install Analysis ToolPak.

4 What are scenarios?

5 List the steps you would use to modify an existing scenario.

Unit 7
Working with macros

Unit time: 45 minutes

Complete this unit, and you'll know how to:

A Create and run macros to automate complex and repetitive tasks.

B Use the Visual Basic Editor to edit a macro.

C Create custom functions.

Topic A: Running and recording a macro

This topic covers the following Microsoft Office Specialist exam objectives.

#	Objective
XL03E-3-2	Setting macro settings
XL03E-5-2	Running macros
XL03E-5-2	Creating macros

What's a macro?

Explanation

You can use macros to automate complex and repetitive tasks. A *macro* is a series of instructions that execute automatically with a single command. For example, you can create a macro to format a worksheet or to print a report. You can use the macros already available in Excel or create your own. To make macros more convenient to use, you can assign them to toolbar buttons.

Run macros

To run a macro, choose Tools, Macro, Macros to open the Macro dialog box. Select the macro of your choice, and click the Run button.

Macro security levels

Macros might contain viruses. You can protect your workbook by setting a macro security level. The security levels available are:

- **High** — Disables macros when you open a workbook.
- **Medium** — Prompts you to either enable or disable macros.
- **Low** — Enables macros automatically when you open a workbook.

To set the macro security level, choose Tools, Macro, Security to open the Security dialog box. On the Security Level tab, select the desired level, and click OK.

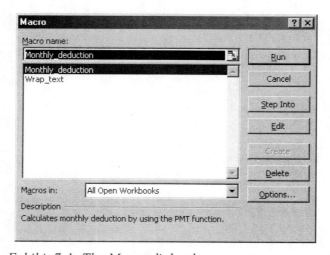

Exhibit 7-1: The Macro dialog box

Do it!

A-1:   Running a macro

Here's how	Here's why
1 Open Running macros	From the current unit folder. If a message box appears prompting you to either enable or disable the macros, click Enable Macros.
2 Save the workbook as **My running macros**	In the current unit folder.
3 Select D4	You'll run the Wrap_text macro to wrap the text in the selected cell.
Choose **Tools**, **Macro**, **Macros...**	To open the Macro dialog box, which displays the names of available macros, as shown in Exhibit 7-1.
From the Macro name list, select **Wrap_text**	
Click **Run**	To run the macro. Notice that the text in the cell is wrapped and appears in multiple lines.
4 Select E4	You'll run the macro in this cell by using the shortcut key.
Press (CTRL) + (SHIFT) + (W)	The text appears on multiple lines in E4.
5 Select E5	
Run the Monthly_deduction macro	(Use the Macro dialog box.) The monthly deduction amount appears in E5.
Select E5	The formula for the PMT function appears in the Formula bar. This formula was entered by the macro you just ran.
6 Display the monthly deduction for James Overmire in E6	Use the shortcut key Ctrl+Shift+M to run the Monthly_deduction macro.
7 Update and close the workbook	

Record macros

To create a macro, you can either write macros from scratch, which can be considered programming, or you can have Excel record the actions you perform. Recording is less efficient, but much easier.

To record a macro:

1 Choose Tools, Macro, Record New Macro to open the Record Macro dialog box.

2 Specify a name for the macro and a shortcut key. Macro names must begin with a letter and can include letters, numbers, and underscores. Spaces can't be included.

3 Click OK to start recording the macro.

4 Perform the actions you want to include in the macro. As you work, Excel records the sequence of steps.

5 When you're finished, click the Stop Recording button on the Stop Recording toolbar.

A-2: Recording a macro

Here's how	Here's why
1 Open Macros	You'll record a macro to calculate the monthly deduction for employees.
2 Save the workbook as **My macros**	
3 Select E5	This cell will contain the formula for calculating the deduction. When you want a macro to be associated with a particular cell, select that cell before turning on the recorder.
Choose **Tools**, **Macro**, **Record New Macro...**	To open the Record Macro dialog box.
4 In the Macro name box, enter **Deduction**	
In the Shortcut key box, type **D**	To define the shortcut key for the Deduction macro as Ctrl+Shift+D.
In the Store macro in list, verify that This Workbook is selected	To specify that the macro will be stored in only the active workbook.
Edit the Description box to read **Calculates monthly deduction**	
5 Click **OK**	
	The Stop Recording toolbar appears. The complete title of the toolbar is not visible.

6	Click	(The Relative Reference button is on the Stop Recording toolbar.) To set the macro recorder to record relative cell references. This way, any movements of the cell pointer will be recorded relative to the position of the active cell.
7	Enter **=PMT(10%/12,D5,-C5)**	This is the action to be recorded. The monthly deduction amount appears in E5, and the active cell has moved down by one row to E6.
8	Click	(The Stop Recording button is on the Stop Recording toolbar.) To stop recording and hide the Stop Recording toolbar. The value in E5 is $1,816.62.
9	Select E6	If necessary.
	Run the **Deduction** macro	(Use the shortcut key Ctrl+Shift+D.) The value in E6 is $1,168.07.
10	Update the workbook	

Assign macros to buttons

Explanation

There are several ways to run a macro. One of them is to assign a macro to a button in a worksheet. After assigning the macro to a button, you can run it by clicking that button.

To assign a macro to a button:

1 Display the Forms toolbar, if necessary.

2 On the Forms toolbar, click the Button tool.

3 Drag on the worksheet to draw a button. The Assign Macro dialog box will open.

4 From the Macro name list, select the name of the macro you want to assign to the button. Click OK to close the dialog box.

5 Edit the text on the button to reflect the function of the macro.

6 Deselect the button.

Do it!   **A-3:   Assigning a macro to a button**

Here's how	Here's why
1 Display the Forms toolbar	Choose View, Toolbars, Forms.
2 Click [button]	(The Button tool is on the Forms toolbar.) You'll draw a rectangle on the worksheet.
Draw as shown	

	E	F	G
	Monthly deduction		
	$1,816.62		
	$1,168.07		

To create a button and open the Assign Macro dialog box. The Deduction macro appears in the Macro name list.

Here's how	Here's why
3 From the Macro name list, select **Deduction**	
Click **OK**	
4 Edit the button caption to read **Calculate monthly deduction**	Select the text on the button, and enter the new caption.
5 Select E7	
Click **Calculate monthly deduction**	The shape of the pointer changes to a hand when you point to the button. The monthly deduction for Annie Philips appears in E7 as $3,428.72.
6 Close the Forms toolbar	
7 Update the workbook	

Topic B: Working with VBA code

This topic covers the following Microsoft Office Specialist exam objective.

#	Objective
XL03E-5-2	Editing macros using the Visual Basic Editor

What is VBA code?

Explanation

Excel saves the steps in a macro as Visual Basic for Applications (VBA) code. You can view and edit the code of a macro with the Visual Basic Editor.

VBA code is stored in special sheets called modules. A *module* might contain one or more Sub procedures. A *Sub procedure* contains the code which, when executed, performs a sequence of steps.

Examine VBA code

VBA code consists of statements and comments. *Statements* are instructions that perform certain actions. *Comments* are non-executable lines of code used to describe the macro.

Comments always begin with a single apostrophe. The following table describes the components of a statement:

Item	Description
Keywords	Special VBA terms that, by default, appear in blue. For example, the Sub keyword marks the beginning of a Sub procedure, and the End Sub keyword marks the end of a Sub procedure.
Variables	Used to store values. For example, you can use variables to store the results of a formula.
Operators	Used just as they are in a worksheet. Operators can be arithmetic (+, -, /, *) or comparison (=, >, <).
Procedure call	A statement that calls a procedure from another procedure. You can do this by inserting the name of the first procedure into the second procedure.

Observe a VBA code module

To observe a VBA code module, open the Macro dialog box. Then, click the Edit button to open the Microsoft Visual Basic window.

Do it!

B-1: Observing a VBA code module

Here's how	Here's why
1 Choose **Tools**, **Macro**, **Macros...**	To open the Macro dialog box. By default, Deduction is selected in the Macro name list.
Click **Edit**	To open the Microsoft Visual Basic window. The name of the workbook appears in the Title bar.
Observe the Code window	This window displays the code of the Deduction macro.
2 Observe the first line in the Code window	`Sub Deduction()` The Sub keyword marks the beginning of the macro. Keywords appear as blue text.
Observe the last line in the Code window	`End Sub` The End Sub keyword marks the end of the macro.

3 Observe the comments	`' Deduction Macro`
	`' Calculates monthly deduction`
	`'`
	`' Keyboard Shortcut: Ctrl+Shift+D`
	
	Comments begin with a single apostrophe and describe the macro. By default, they appear as green text.

Observe the second comment	`' Deduction Macro` This comment indicates the name of the macro.
Observe the third comment	`' Calculates monthly deduction` This comment displays the description you entered in the Record Macro dialog box.
4 Observe the statements	Statements appear in black and instruct Excel to perform a sequence of actions. The statements are located between the Sub and End Sub keywords.
Observe the first statement	This statement enters the PMT function into the active cell. In this formula, "RC[-1]" refers to the cell that is one column to the left of the active cell, and "-RC[-2]" refers to the cell that is two columns to the left of the active cell.
Observe the second statement	`ActiveCell.Offset(1, 0).Range("A1").Select` This statement selects the cell directly below the active cell.

Edit VBA code

Explanation

Sometimes you might need to edit the code of a macro. For example, say you have a macro that calculates the monthly deduction at an interest rate of 12%, and you want to change the interest rate to 11%. Instead of recording a new macro, you can edit the VBA code of the existing macro to reflect the change.

You can edit macro code in Visual Basic Editor. Make sure to save the macro after you've made any necessary changes.

Do it!

B-2: Editing VBA code

Here's how	Here's why
1 Edit the first argument in the PMT function to read **11%/12**	`"=PMT(11%/12,RC[-1],-RC[-2])"`
2 Update and close the Microsoft Visual Basic window	Choose File, Save My macros.xls.
3 Select E5, and run the Deduction macro	(Click the Calculate monthly deduction button in the worksheet.) The value in the cell changes to $1858.98.
4 Update the workbook	

Topic C: Function procedures

Explanation

A *Function procedure* is similar to a Sub procedure except that it returns a value on execution. All the built-in functions of Excel, such as SUM and AVERAGE, are written by using Function procedures.

You can also create functions to meet your specific needs. Such functions are called *custom functions*. For example, you can create a function that calculates commissions for salespeople based on their total sales.

Create custom functions

You create custom functions in a Visual Basic module. In a custom function, you can include mathematical expressions, built-in Excel functions, and Visual Basic code. You can create custom functions to work with text, numbers, or dates.

You use custom functions in the same way that you use built-in functions. You can also supply values to a custom function. That function then performs calculations on those values and returns a result.

Parts of a custom function

Examine the following code:

```
Function Profit(sales, cost)
Profit=sales-cost
End Function
```

Here, the Function keyword marks the beginning of the function. Profit is the name of the function, and the End Function keyword marks the termination of the function.

Arguments are the values that a function uses for calculations. Arguments are specified in parentheses after the function name. In the preceding code, sales and cost are the arguments of the Profit function.

A *return value* is the value returned by a function after execution. You specify the return value by equating the function name to the value it must return. This is shown in the second statement of the preceding code.

Do it!

C-1: Creating a custom function

Here's how	Here's why
1 Activate the Function sheet	
2 Choose **Tools**, **Macro**, **Visual Basic Editor**	To open the Microsoft Visual Basic window.
3 Choose **Insert**, **Module**	Microsoft Visual Basic - My macros.xls - [Module2 (Code)]
	To add a module sheet. In the title bar, Module2 indicates that this is the second module in the My macros workbook.
4 Place the insertion point in the Code window	If necessary.
5 Enter the following code:	

```
Function MyFunction(sales2004, sales2003)
```

	This code defines a function named MyFunction in which sales2004 and sales2003 are the arguments.
Press ⏎ ENTER	To move to the next row. The keyword End Function appears automatically at the end.
6 Enter the following code:	

```
MyFunction=(sales2004-sales2003)/sales2003*100
```

	This code calculates the percent increase in sales and returns the result.
7 Update the code	Choose File, Save My macros.xls.
Close the Microsoft Visual Basic window	
8 Switch to Excel	If necessary.
In D5, enter **=MyFunction(C5,B5)**	The percent increase in sales for Mary Smith appears in D5 as 53.04.
9 Update and close the workbook	

Unit summary: Working with macros

Topic A   In this topic, you learned how to **record** and **run a macro**. You learned that macros perform tasks automatically and can be created to meet your specific needs. Then, you learned how to **assign a macro to a button** and run it by clicking that button.

Topic B   In this topic, you learned that macros are saved as VBA code, and you examined some **VBA code**. Then, you learned how to **edit the code** of a macro. You learned how to update a macro by editing its VBA code.

Topic C   In this topic, you learned how to create a **custom function**. You learned that custom functions are used to perform calculations when built-in functions are not available.

Independent practice activity

1 Open Macros practice. (The Macros worksheet contains two scenarios: Original and Cost of sales.)

2 Save the workbook as **My macros practice**.

3 Record a macro named **Display_cost_of_sales** that has Ctrl+Shift+C as its shortcut key. This macro should show the Cost of sales scenario. (*Hint:* Start recording the macro. Choose Tools, Scenarios; select Cost of sales; and click Show. Click Close; then stop recording the macro.)

4 Record a macro named **Display_original** that has Ctrl+Shift+O as its shortcut key. This macro should show the Original scenario.

5 Run the Display_cost_of_sales macro. Run the Display_original macro.

6 Change the name of the Cost of sales scenario to Decreased cost of sales. (*Hint:* Open the Scenario Manager dialog box, select Cost of sales from the Scenarios list, and click Edit.)

7 Edit the VBA code of the Display_cost_of_sales macro to show the Decreased cost of sales scenario. Close the Microsoft Visual Basic window. (*Hint:* Choose Tools, Macro, Macros. In the Display_cost_of_sales macro, edit the argument of the ActiveSheet.Scenarios function to read Decreased cost of sales.)

8 Run the edited macro.

9 Update the workbook and close it.

Review questions

1 What is a macro?

2 List two ways to create a macro.

3 In what type of code, or language, does Excel save macros? Where can you view and edit this code?

4 What is unique about a Function procedure?

5 How do you specify a return value in a function?

Unit 8

Interactive Web pages

Unit time: 30 minutes

Complete this unit, and you'll know how to:

A Publish and maintain an Excel-based interactive Web page.

B Add a PivotTable to a Web page so that users can interact with the data.

Topic A: Creating interactive Web spreadsheets

Explanation

You can use the publishing and saving features of Excel to display an entire workbook or part of a workbook on a Web page. By default, Excel displays a static Web page on which users cannot manipulate data. However, you can make a Web page interactive to allow users to change information.

Publish interactive Web pages

You add interactivity to your Excel worksheets when you publish them on the Web. To interact with the published data, you need to have Microsoft Office Web Components installed. These components are a standard feature of the Internet Explorer 5.0 browser.

You should always test Web pages in all browsers that you think people are likely to use when accessing your pages. It's best to apply only those features that work with all the browsers your audience might use.

To publish an interactive Web page:

1 Open the workbook that contains the data you want to publish.

2 Choose File, Save as Web Page to open the Save As dialog box.

3 Specify whether you want to save the entire workbook or just the active worksheet as the data source.

4 Check Add interactivity.

5 In the File name box, specify the name of the Web page.

6 Click Publish to open the Publish as Web Page dialog box, as shown in Exhibit 8-1.

7 If you want the Web page to automatically open in a browser as soon as the page is published, check Open published web page in browser.

8 Click Publish.

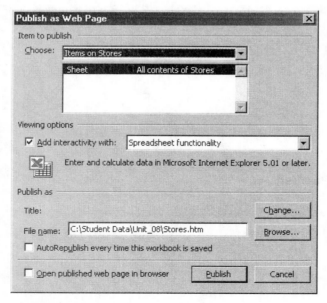

Exhibit 8-1: The Publish as Web Page dialog box

Do it!   **A-1:   Publishing an interactive Web page**

Here's how	Here's why
1 Open Advanced Web	(From the current unit folder.) This workbook contains three worksheets. Stores is the active sheet.
2 Save the workbook as **My advanced Web**	In the current unit folder.
3 Choose **File, Web Page Preview**	To display the worksheet as a Web page in Internet Explorer. You cannot change the data on this Web page because by default, Excel publishes a static Web page.
Close Internet Explorer	
4 Choose **File, Save as Web Page...**	To open the Save As dialog box.
From the Save as type list, select **Web Page**	(If necessary.) To save the worksheet as a Web page that can be viewed in a browser.
In the Save area, select **Selection: Sheet**	To specify that you want to publish the active worksheet instead of the entire workbook.
Check **Add interactivity**	To specify that users can change the data on the Web page.
Edit the File name box to read **Stores**	This will be the name of the Web page. Excel will automatically add the .htm file extension to this name.
5 Click **Publish**	To open the Publish as Web Page dialog box, as shown in Exhibit 8-1.
In the Choose list, verify that Items on Stores is selected	This will show all the items in the Stores worksheet. You can also choose to publish a range of cells, previously published items, or items in another sheet in this workbook.
Check **Open published web page in browser**	(If necessary.) This will automatically display the Web page in a browser after you publish it.
Click **Publish**	To publish the worksheet as a Web page. This will open the published worksheet in Internet Explorer.

6	Maximize the Internet Explorer window	(If necessary.) The worksheet appears on the Web page.
	Observe the toolbar	(In the upper region of the Web page.)

		This is the Spreadsheet toolbar. You can use it to interact with the published data. However, the changes made in the Web page will not be reflected in the original Excel worksheet. To save the changes, you can export the Web page to Excel and save it with another name or in another location.
7	Edit A6 to read **Hayward**	In Internet Explorer.
	Press ⏎ ENTER	This will display the details of the store in Hayward.
8	Close Internet Explorer	
9	Observe A6:D6	(In Excel.) The data in these cells hasn't changed.
10	Update the workbook	

Maintain Excel-based Web pages

Explanation

After publishing a workbook, you might need to change the data in the source workbook. To reflect these changes on the Web page, you save the modified workbook and then republish the data by using the Save as Web Page command.

Do it!

A-2: Maintaining an Excel-based Web page

Here's how	Here's why
1 Verify that the Stores sheet is activated	You'll change the information in this worksheet and republish it on the Stores Web page.
2 In D10, enter **Shane Johnson**	
Update the workbook	
3 Choose **File**, **Save as Web Page…**	To open the Save As dialog box. The File name box displays the name of the workbook as the default name. Notice that the Save as type list is available.
In the Save area, select **Republish: Sheet**	This will republish the worksheet data on the Stores Web page.
Verify that Add interactivity is checked	
Observe the dialog box	The File name box displays Stores.htm. Notice that the Save as type list is no longer available.
4 Click **Publish**	To open the Publish as Web Page dialog box.
In the Choose list, verify that Previously published items is selected	This will republish the same worksheet items that you published earlier.
5 Click **Publish**	This opens the revised Stores Web page in Internet Explorer and displays the current worksheet data.
Observe D10	(In Internet Explorer. You might need to scroll through the workbook to view the name.) It now contains Shane Johnson.
Close Internet Explorer	
6 Update the workbook	

Topic B: Publishing PivotTables on the Web

Explanation

You can publish a PivotTable on the Web so that users can interact with the data. All the basic functions of a PivotTable are supported on the Web.

Publish a PivotTable on a Web page

To publish a PivotTable on a Web page:
1   Select the entire PivotTable.
2   Choose File, Save as Web Page to open the Save As dialog box.
3   Select the Selection: PivotTable option, and check Add interactivity.
4   Click Publish to open the Publish as Web Page dialog box.
5   Make any selections you want, and then click Publish.

Add a field to a PivotTable by using a Web browser

You can add fields to your PivotTable by using a Web browser. To do so:
1   Publish the PivotTable to the Web.
2   On the Spreadsheet toolbar in your Web browser, click the Field List button to open the PivotTable Field List window.
3   Drag the field you want to add to the relevant location in the PivotTable. You can also select the field you want to add, select a location from the list in the lower region of the PivotTable Field List dialog box, and click Add To.

Do it!

B-1:   Using a PivotTable on a Web page

Here's how	Here's why
1 Activate the Pivot sheet	You'll publish the PivotTable in this worksheet as a Web page.
2 Select A4	(This cell is within the PivotTable layout.) The PivotTable Field List window appears.
3 Click as shown	
	(On the PivotTable toolbar.) To display a menu.
Choose **Select**, **Entire Table**	To select the entire PivotTable.
4 Choose **File**, **Save as Web Page...**	To open the Save As dialog box.
From the Save as type list, select **Web Page**	(If necessary.) To save the PivotTable as a Web page.
In the Save area, select **Selection: PivotTable**	To specify that you want to publish the PivotTable.

5	Check **Add interactivity**	To specify that users can change the data on the Web page.
	Edit the File name box to read **Sales PivotTable**	To specify the name of the Web page.
6	Click **Publish**	To open the Publish as Web Page dialog box.
	In the Choose list, verify that Items on Pivot is selected	
	Under Item to publish, observe the second list	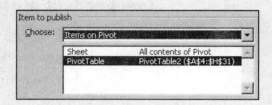

This list gives you the option of publishing all contents of the Pivot worksheet or just the PivotTable. PivotTable is the default selection.

	Click **Publish**	As Excel publishes the data, Internet Explorer displays progress messages.
7	Maximize the Internet Explorer window	(If necessary.) You'll see the PivotTable on the Web page.
8	Display the sales of only the North region	(In the Region list, clear all options except North.) The PivotTable is recalculated based on the changed data.
	Make Region the page field	(Drag Region to Drop Filter Fields Here.) Page fields are called *filter fields* on a Web page.
9	Click 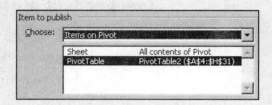	(The Field List button is on the Spreadsheet toolbar.) To display the PivotTable Field List window. It displays the column headings of the source data. You can drag fields from this window to the PivotTable to change the view.
	Close the PivotTable Field List window	
	Close Internet Explorer	
10	Update and close the workbook	

Unit summary: Interactive Web pages

Topic A In this topic, you learned about **publishing** a workbook or part of a workbook as a **Web page**. Next, you learned that you can change the source data and **republish** the Web page to reflect those changes.

Topic B In this topic, you learned how to **publish a PivotTable** as a Web page. You learned that you can use a Web browser to **add fields** to the PivotTable after publishing it.

Independent practice activity

1 Open Advanced Web practice.

2 Save the workbook as **My advanced Web practice**.

3 Publish the Employee worksheet as an interactive Web page, and name it **My employee**.

4 In Excel, edit E10 to read **Accounting**. Republish the worksheet to reflect this change on the Web page.

5 Activate the Pivot worksheet.

6 Publish the PivotTable as an interactive Web page, and name it **My pivot**.

7 Make Year the page field.

8 Move Quarter to be a column field. Compare your worksheet to Exhibit 8-2.

9 Close Internet Explorer.

10 Update and close the workbook.

11 Close Excel.

	A	B	C	D	E	F	G	H
3	Sum of Sales		Year					
4	Product	Quarter	1996	1997	1998	1999	2000	Grand Total
5	Anise Seeds	Qtr1	26000	29380	34840	41010	48326	179556
6		Qtr2	33112	37417	44370	52228	61545	228671
7		Qtr3	28874	32628	38691	45543	53668	199404
8		Qtr4	27220	30759	36475	42934	50594	187981
9	Anise Seeds Total		115206	130183	154376	181714	214133	795613
10	Basil Leaf	Qtr1	13800	15594	18492	21767	25650	95303
11		Qtr2	15080	17040	20207	23786	28029	104142
12		Qtr3	12821	14488	17180	20223	23830	88542
13		Qtr4	16363	18490	21926	25809	30414	113003
14	Basil Leaf Total		58064	65612	77806	91584	107924	400990
15	Cassia	Qtr1	45000	50850	60300	70979	83642	310770
16		Qtr2	43983	49701	58937	69374	81751	303747
17		Qtr3	46343	52368	62100	73097	86138	320045
18		Qtr4	45892	51858	61495	72385	85299	316930
19	Cassia Total		181218	204776	242832	285835	336830	1251492

Exhibit 8-2: The Pivot worksheet after step 8 of the Independent Practice Activity

Review questions

1 By default, does Excel display a static Web page or an interactive Web page?

2 To interact with the published data, what do you need to have installed on your computer?

3 You should always test Web pages in all browsers that you think people are likely to use when accessing your pages. True or False?

4 If changes have been made to a worksheet after it's been published, how can you update the Web page?

5 What steps would you use to publish a PivotTable on a Web page?

Unit 9

Using SharePoint services

Unit time: 30 minutes

Complete this unit, and you'll know how to:

A Create a Document Workspace, publish and view a list in SharePoint server, and synchronize a list with SharePoint server.

Topic A: Document Workspaces

Explanation

A *Document Workspace* is a Web site based on Microsoft Windows SharePoint Services. A Document Workspace helps you share documents with project team members, facilitates discussions, and helps members work simultaneously on a single document. Documents are stored in a *document library*, which is a folder of shared files. Members of the Document Workspace can access these files by using a Web browser or the Shared Workspace task pane in Microsoft Office 2003 applications such as Word, PowerPoint, and Excel. The following table lists the features of a Document Workspace:

Feature	Description
Members list	Displays the names of members and their online status. You can also invite other members to work on your document.
Tasks list	Helps you assign jobs to other members or make a to-do list for yourself.
Document library	Stores the shared documents.
Links list	Displays the links available in the Document Workspace.
Dynamic updates	Displays information such as the status of tasks and the online status of members. It also notifies members of updates to the workspace copy of a document.

Create Document Workspaces

You use the Shared Workspace task pane or Microsoft Office Outlook 2003 to create a Document Workspace. You should have the permission to create a Document Workspace at the SharePoint Services site.

Use the Shared Workspace task pane

The Shared Workspace task pane displays information about the SharePoint Services site, such as the members of the workspace and their online status, tasks listed, shared documents, and available hyperlinks. Exhibit 9-1 shows the Shared Workspace task pane.

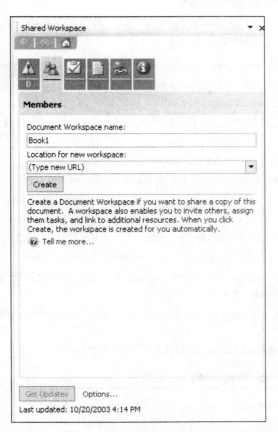

Exhibit 9-1: The Shared Workspace task pane

To create a Document Workspace by using the Shared Workspace task pane:

1   Choose Tools, Shared Workspace to display the Shared Workspace task pane.

2   In the Location for new workspace box, enter the Web address of the SharePoint server.

3   Click the Create button.

Use Microsoft Office Outlook 2003

You can also create a Document Workspace by using Outlook 2003. To do so:

1 Start Microsoft Office Outlook 2003.

2 Choose File, New, Mail Message to open a new Message window.

3 In the To box, enter the e-mail address of the person who wants to be a member of the Document Workspace.

4 In the Cc box, enter the e-mail address of other members who are part of the team.

5 In the Subject box, enter the subject of the message.

6 Choose Insert, File to open the Insert File dialog box.

7 Select the document you want to add to your Document Workspace, and click the Insert button.

8 Click Attachment Options to display the Attachment Options task pane.

9 Under Send attachments as, select Shared attachments.

10 In the Create Document Workspace at box, enter the Web address of the Microsoft Windows SharePoint Services site.

11 Type the message in the message area of the Message window, and click Send.

Do it!

A-1: Creating a Document Workspace

Questions and answers
1 What are the methods to create a Document Workspace?
2 What is a document library?
3 How can you create a Document Workspace by using Outlook 2003?

Publish and view lists on the SharePoint server

Explanation

A list in Excel groups related data in a worksheet. A workbook can contain multiple lists. If you're using a workbook with multiple lists, you can analyze the data in one list independently of the data in other lists. For example, you can sort and filter a single list. You can also share a list by publishing it to the SharePoint Services site. The members of the site can view, edit, or update the list. You can publish a list on the SharePoint Services site only if you have permission to do so.

To publish a list:

1 Select the list in the workbook.
2 Choose Data, List, Publish List to open Step 1 of the Publish List to SharePoint Site Wizard.
3 In the Address box, enter the Web address of the SharePoint server.
4 Check Link to the new SharePoint Services list. This helps you link your list to the list that will be created in the SharePoint site.
5 In the Name box, enter a name for the list.
6 In the Description box, enter a description for the list. Click Next.
7 Specify the data type for the columns in the list, if necessary.
8 Click Finish.

To view a published list:

1 Select the list in the worksheet.
2 Choose Data, List, View List on Server.

Do it!

A-2: Publishing and viewing a list on the SharePoint server

Questions and answers
1 Why do you use a list in a worksheet?
2 You can sort and filter data in a list. True or false?
3 Do you need permission to create a list on the SharePoint Services site?
4 How can you view a published list?

Synchronize lists with the SharePoint server

Explanation

If you link your list with the published list on the SharePoint server, you can synchronize the two lists. You can either publish your changes to the SharePoint list or discard the changes in your list.

To publish the changes in your list to the SharePoint list and include the changes in the SharePoint list in your list, choose Data, List, Synchronize List. You can discard the changes in your list and include the SharePoint list's changes in your list by choosing Data, List, Discard Changes and Refresh.

Do it!

A-3: Synchronizing a list with data on the SharePoint server

Questions and answers

1 Can you synchronize a list in an Excel worksheet with a list published in the SharePoint site?

2 How can you discard the changes in a list?

Unit summary: Using SharePoint services

Topic A
In this topic, you learned how to **create a Document Workspace**. You also learned how to **publish** and **view lists** on the SharePoint server. You learned about **synchronizing lists** with data on the SharePoint server.

Review questions

1 What is a Document Workspace?

2 How do you create a Document Workspace by using the Shared Workspace task pane?

3 How can you analyze a group of data independently of other data in a worksheet?

4 How can you link your list with a SharePoint list?

5 You use Synchronize List to publish the changes in your list to the SharePoint list. True or false?

Appendix A

Smart documents

This appendix covers these additional topics:

A Introduction to smart documents.

Topic A: Discussing smart documents

Explanation

Smart documents are Word 2003 documents or Excel 2003 workbooks with an underlying XML (Extensible Markup Language) schema. These documents or workbooks provide assistance in the Office task pane, allowing you to spend less time looking up information and more time exercising your judgment and creativity. For example, in an Excel worksheet, depending on the selected cell, different types of context-specific help or useful information can be displayed. The task pane can also display calculation fields or hyperlinks to external Web sites.

Using smart documents

Smart documents provide relevant content as you work. Data can be stored in a central repository, making it easily accessible and reusable, increasing productivity, accuracy, and standardization. For example, you can use a smart document to create a sales report. The template of the report might contain fields for the salesperson's name, the region, the sales per quarter, and the total sales. If you convert this template to a smart document, data such as the name and the region can be filled in for you automatically.

It's also possible to program the task pane to provide relevant data, helpful questions, hyperlinks, graphics, and controls such as buttons, check boxes, and option buttons. For example, the task pane can be made to display the sales details of different products while quarterly sales data is being entered.

Smart documents also contain programming logic defining how the file can be used. For example, after entering data in your sales report, you can send it to the sales department by clicking a Submit button on the task pane. If the supervisor in the sales department wants you to change any data, she can send the document back to you along with comments. Otherwise, you will receive an e-mail message confirming that the document has been submitted.

Because smart documents can interact with other Office 2003 applications, you can easily share information. You can send e-mail messages through Outlook from a smart document without starting Outlook.

Creating smart documents

To convert an Excel workbook to a smart document, you use XML expansion packs. An *XML expansion pack* contains components such as XML files and a manifest file with references to these components. A *solution manifest* is a file that contains the locations of the files used in the smart document. The solution manifest is an XML file that connects your document to XML components such as the XML schema. You store the manifest file along with the code and supporting XML files on a server. When you open a smart document, the manifest file checks for the necessary data and downloads the required files to ensure that the document functions properly.

You use the smart document Application Program Interface (API) to write the code that controls the smart document. The code can be written in Visual Basic, Visual Basic .Net, C# .Net, or Visual C++. This code either manipulates the document or interacts with the server to retrieve data. You can write code to perform tasks such as retrieving data from the server or sending the document to the relevant person. The same code can be used for other applications as well.

Distributing smart documents

You can distribute your smart documents over an intranet or the Internet by using XML Web services or a Web site based on SharePoint Team Services. You install a smart document solution by opening it. The Document Actions task pane will appear automatically. This task pane displays tools and data for using the smart document. The document is automatically updated from the server, ensuring that you are working with the latest version. Smart document solutions implement high security standards. Therefore, you can download the solutions only from trusted sites.

Appendix B

Microsoft Office Specialist exam objectives maps

This appendix covers these additional topics:

A Excel 2003 Specialist exam objectives with references to corresponding material in ILT Series courseware.

B Excel 2003 Expert exam objectives with references to corresponding material in ILT Series courseware.

Topic A: Specialist exam objectives

Explanation

The following table lists all Excel 2003 Specialist exam objectives and provides references to the conceptual material and activities that teach each objective.

Objective	Course level	Conceptual information	Supporting activities
Entering, editing, and clearing text, numbers and symbols in cells	Basic	Unit 2, Topic B, pp 4, 6 Unit 2, Topic C, pp 10-11	B-1, B-2 C-1
Fill series content using the fill handle tool	Basic	Unit 3, Topic B, p 14	B-3
Finding and modifying or replacing cell content or formatting	Basic	Unit 2, Topic B, p 8 Unit 5, Topic D, p 24	B-3 D-3
Navigate to specific content (e.g., Go To)	Basic	Unit 1, Topic D, p 16	D-2
Locating supporting information in local reference materials or on the Internet using the Research tool	Basic	Unit 1, Topic C, pp 8, 10-11 Unit 6, Topic A, p 4	C-1, C-2, C-3 A-2
Using the Research tool to select and insert supporting text-based information	Basic	Unit 6, Topic A, p 4	A-2
Inserting, positioning, and sizing graphics	Intermediate	Unit 6, Topic C, pp 10, 14	C-1, C-3
Filtering lists using AutoFilter	Intermediate	Unit 5, Topic B, p 6	B-3
Sorting lists	Intermediate	Unit 5, Topic B, pp 3-4	B-1, B-2
Creating and editing formulas	Basic	Unit 2, Topic C, pp 10-13	C-1, C-2, C-3
Entering a range within a formula by dragging	Basic	Unit 4, Topic A, p 5	A-2
Using references (absolute and relative)	Basic	Unit 3, Topic B, p 12 Unit 3, Topic C, pp 15, 17	B-2 C-1, C-2
Creating formulas using the following function categories: Statistical, Date and Time, Financial, and Logical (e.g., Sum, Min, Max, Date or Now, PMT, IF, Average)	Basic	Unit 4, Topic A, pp 2-3, 5-6 Unit 4, Topic C, pp 10, 12-13	A-1, A-2, A-3 C-1, C-2, C-3
	Intermediate	Unit 4, Topic C, pp 16, 18	C-2, C-3
	Advanced	Unit 1, Topic B, p 10 Unit 1, Topic D, p 18	B-1 D-1
Creating, modifying, and positioning diagrams and charts based on data contained in the active workbook	Basic	Unit 7, Topic A, pp 2, 6 Unit 7, Topic B, pp 8, 12	A-1, A-3 B-1, B-3
	Intermediate	Unit 6, Topic C, p 14	C-3
Formatting cells	Basic	Unit 5, Topic A, p 5	A-3

Objective	Course level	Conceptual information	Supporting activities
Applying AutoFormats to cells and cell ranges	Basic	Unit 5, Topic D, p 22	D-2
Applying styles (e.g., applying a style from the Format>Style list)	Intermediate	Unit 4, Topic D, pp 19, 21	D-2
Modifying height and width	Basic	Unit 5, Topic B, p 7	B-1
Inserting and deleting, hiding and unhiding rows and columns	Basic	Unit 3, Topic D, pp 20-21	D-2, D-3
	Intermediate	Unit 1, Topic B, p 6	B-1
Modifying alignment	Basic	Unit 5, Topic B, p 9	B-2
Formatting tab color, sheet name, and background	Intermediate	Unit 2, Topic A, p 4 Unit 4, Topic A, p 4	A-2 A-2
Hiding and unhiding worksheets	Intermediate	Unit 1, Topic B, p 6	B-1
Adding and editing comments attached to worksheet cells	Intermediate	Unit 7, Topic B, p 7	B-2
Creating a workbook from a template	Intermediate	Unit 8, Topic A, pp 2-3, 6	A-1, A-2
Inserting and deleting selected cells	Basic	Unit 3, Topic D, pp 18, 21	D-1, D-3
Cutting, copying and pasting/pasting special selected cells	Basic	Unit 3, Topic A, pp 2, 4 Unit 5, Topic B, p 7	A-1, A-2
Moving selected cells	Basic	Unit 3, Topic A, pp 2, 6	A-1, A-3
Inserting and editing hyperlinks	Basic	Unit 8, Topic B, p 6	B-1
Inserting worksheets into a workbook	Intermediate	Unit 2, Topic A, p 6	A-3
Deleting worksheets from a workbook	Intermediate	Unit 2, Topic A, p 6	A-3
Repositioning worksheets in a workbook	Intermediate	Unit 2, Topic A, p 6	A-3
Previewing print and Web pages	Basic	Unit 6, Topic A, p 5 Unit 8, Topic A, p 2	A-3 A-1
Previewing page breaks	Intermediate	Unit 1, Topic C, p 14	C-3
Splitting and arranging workbooks	Intermediate	Unit 2, Topic E, p 21	E-1
Splitting, freezing/unfreezing, arranging and hiding/unhiding workbooks	Intermediate	Unit 1, Topic A, pp 4-5 Unit 2, Topic E, p 21	A-2, A-3
Setting print areas	Basic	Unit 6, Topic C, p 17	C-2
Modifying worksheet orientation	Basic	Unit 6, Topic B, p 7	B-1
Adding headers and footers to worksheets	Basic	Unit 6, Topic B, p 11	B-3
Viewing and modifying page breaks	Intermediate	Unit 1, Topic C, pp 13-14	C-2, C-3

Objective	Course level	Conceptual information	Supporting activities
Setting Page Setup options for printing (e.g.; margins, print area, rows/columns to repeat)	Basic	Unit 6, Topic B, pp 9, 13	B-2, B-4
Printing selections, worksheets, and workbooks	Basic	Unit 6, Topic C, pp 15, 17	C-1, C-2
Creating and using folders for workbook storage	Basic	Unit 2, Topic D, pp 14-15	D-1
Renaming folders	Basic	Unit 2, Topic D, pp 14	
Converting files to different file formats for transportability (e.g., .csv, .txt)	Advanced	Unit 5, Topic A, p 2	A-1
Saving selections, worksheets or workbooks as Web pages	Basic	Unit 8, Topic A, pp 2, 4	A-1, A-2

Topic B: Expert exam objectives

Explanation

The following table lists all Excel 2003 Expert exam objectives and provides references to the conceptual material and activities that teach each objective.

Objective	Course level	Conceptual information	Supporting activities
Adding subtotals to worksheet data	Advanced	Unit 3, Topic A, p 2	A-1
Creating and applying advanced filters	Intermediate	Unit 5, Topic C, pp 7-9	C-1, C-2
Grouping and outlining data	Intermediate	Unit 1, Topic B, pp 8-9	B-2
Adding data validation criteria to cells	Advanced	Unit 3, Topic B, pp 5, 7	B-1, B-2
Creating and modifying list ranges	Intermediate	Unit 5, Topic C, p 12	C-3
Managing scenarios	Advanced	Unit 6, Topic C, pp 11, 14-15	C-1, C-2, C-3
Projecting values using analysis tools (e.g., Analysis ToolPak)	Advanced	Unit 6, Topic B, pp 7-8, 10	B-2
Performing What-If analysis	Advanced	Unit 6, Topic A, pp 2, 4	A-1, A-2
Using the Solver add-in	Advanced	Unit 6, Topic A, p 4	A-2
Creating PivotTable Reports and PivotChart Reports	Advanced	Unit 4, Topic A, pp 2-3 Unit 4, Topic D, p 14	A-1 D-1
Using Lookup and Reference functions (e.g., HLOOKUP, VLOOKUP)	Advanced	Unit 2, Topic A, pp 2, 4-5 Unit 2, Topic B, pp 6, 8	A-1, A-2, A-3 B-1, B-2
Creating and editing Database functions (e.g., DSUM, DAVERAGE)	Advanced	Unit 3, Topic C, pp 10-11, 13	C-1, C-2
Tracing formula precedents	Intermediate	Unit 7, Topic A, p 2	A-1
Tracing formula dependents	Intermediate	Unit 7, Topic A, p 2	A-1
Tracing formula errors	Intermediate	Unit 7, Topic A, p 4	A-2
Using Error Checking	Intermediate	Unit 7, Topic A, p 4	A-2
Circling invalid data	Advanced	Unit 3, Topic B, p 5	
Using Evaluate formulas	Advanced	Unit 1, Topic C, p 15	C-2
Using cell Watch	Intermediate	Unit 2, Topic B, p 11	B-2
Naming one or more cell ranges	Advanced	Unit 1, Topic A, pp 2, 6, 8	A-1, A-2, A-3
Using a named range reference in a formula	Advanced	Unit 1, Topic A, p 8	A-3

Objective	Course level	Conceptual information	Supporting activities
Adding, modifying and deleting maps	Advanced	Unit 5, Topic B, pp 6-7, 12	B-1, B-4
Managing elements and attributes in XML workbooks (e.g., adding, modifying, deleting, cutting, copying)	Advanced	Unit 5, Topic B, pp 6-7, 10	B-1, B-3
Defining XML options (e.g., applying XML view options)	Advanced	Unit 5, Topic B, pp 6-7	B-1
Creating and applying custom number formats	Intermediate	Unit 4, Topic B, p 10	B-3
Using conditional formatting	Basic	Unit 5, Topic C, p 18	C-3
Using cropping and rotating tools	Intermediate	Unit 6, Topic C, p 14	C-3
Controlling image contrast and brightness	Intermediate	Unit 6, Topic C, p 14	C-3
Scaling and resizing graphics	Intermediate	Unit 6, Topic C, p 14	C-3
Applying formats to charts and diagrams (e.g., data series, plot area)	Basic	Unit 7, Topic B, p 10	B-2
Adding protection to cells, worksheets and workbooks	Intermediate	Unit 7, Topic C, pp 12-14	C-1, C-2
Using digital signatures to authenticate workbooks	Intermediate	Unit 7, Topic C, p 15	C-3
Setting passwords	Intermediate	Unit 7, Topic C, p 13	C-1
Setting macro settings	Advanced	Unit 7, Topic A, pp 2, 6	A-3
Creating and modifying shared workbooks	Intermediate	Unit 7, Topic D, pp 16-17	D-1
Merging multiple versions of the same workbook	Intermediate	Unit 7, Topic D, p 19	D-2
Tracking changes	Intermediate	Unit 7, Topic D, p 22	D-3
Accepting and rejecting changes	Intermediate	Unit 7, Topic D, p 22	D-3
Bringing information into Excel from external sources	Advanced	Unit 5, Topic C, p 13	C-1
Linking to Web page data	Advanced	Unit 5, Topic C, pp 16-17	C-3
Exporting structured data from Excel	Advanced	Unit 5, Topic B, p 10	B-3
Publishing Web-based worksheets	Basic	Unit 8, Topic A, p 4	A-2
Creating a workbook template	Intermediate	Unit 8, Topic B, p 7	B-1
Creating a new workbook based upon a user-defined template	Intermediate	Unit 8, Topic B, p 7	B-1

Objective	Course level	Conceptual information	Supporting activities
Editing a workbook template	Intermediate	Unit 8, Topic B, p 9	B-2
Consolidating data from two or more worksheets	Intermediate	Unit 2, Topic C, pp 12-13	C-1
Managing workbook properties (e.g., summary data)	Intermediate	Unit 7, Topic B, p 7	B-2
Adding and removing buttons from toolbars	Intermediate	Unit 3, Topic B, p 15	B-3
Adding custom menus	Intermediate	Unit 3, Topic B, p 18	B-4
Creating macros	Advanced	Unit 7, Topic A, p 4	A-2
Editing macros using the Visual Basic Editor	Advanced	Unit 7, Topic B, p 10	B-2
Running macros	Advanced	Unit 7, Topic A, p 2	A-1
Modifying default font settings	Intermediate	Unit 3, Topic A, p 5	A-2
Setting the default number of worksheets	Intermediate	Unit 3, Topic A, p 5	
Changing the default file location for templates	Intermediate	Unit 8, Topic B, p 10	B-3

Course summary

This summary contains information to help you bring the course to a successful conclusion. Using this information, you will be able to:

A Use the summary text to reinforce what you've learned in class.

B Determine the next courses in this series (if any), as well as any other resources that might help you continue to learn about Excel 2003.

Topic A: Course summary

Use the following summary text to reinforce what you've learned in class.

Unit summaries

Unit 1

In this unit, you learned how to use **named ranges** to make formulas easier to understand. Next, you learned how to use the **IF** and **SUMIF** functions to evaluate data on the basis of specified criteria. Then, you learned how to round off a number by using the **ROUND** function. Finally, you learned how to use the **PMT** function to calculate the periodic payment for a loan.

Unit 2

In this unit, you learned how to use **lookup functions** to find a specific value in a worksheet. You learned how to use **VLOOKUP** to search for a value in a list that is arranged vertically. Next, you learned how to use the **MATCH** function to find the relative position of a value in a range. You also learned how to use the **INDEX** function to find a value in a range by specifying a row and column number. Finally, you learned how to create **one-variable** and **two-variable data tables** to project values.

Unit 3

In this unit, you learned how to create automatic **subtotals** to summarize data in a worksheet. Next, you learned how to use the **Data Validation** feature to validate the data entered in cells. Then, you learned how to use **database functions** to summarize values that meet complex criteria. Finally, you learned how to use a **data form** to enter data in a list.

Unit 4

In this unit, you learned how to **create a PivotTable** by using the PivotTable and PivotChart Wizard. Next, you learned how to display different views of data by moving fields and by hiding and showing details in the PivotTable. Then, you learned how to add formatting to PivotTable data by changing **field settings**. Finally, you learned how to create **PivotCharts** to graphically display data from the PivotTable.

Unit 5

In this unit, you learned how to **export data** from Excel to a text file. You learned how to **import data** from a text file into an Excel workbook. Next, you learned how to import and export **XML data** by using the XML Source task pane. Finally, you learned how to use **Microsoft Query** to retrieve data from an Access database. You also learned how to use the **Web query** feature to get data from a Web page.

Unit 6

In this unit, you learned how to use **Goal Seek** and **Solver** to meet a target output for a formula by adjusting the values of input cells. Next, you learned how to install and use the **Analysis ToolPak**. Then, you learned how to create **scenarios** to save various sets of values in a worksheet. Finally, you learned how to create **views** to save different sets of worksheet display and print settings.

Unit 7

In this unit, you learned how to **run a macro** that automatically performed tasks for you. You also learned how to **record a macro**, as well as how to **assign a macro to a button** so that users can run the macro by clicking the button. Next, you learned how to **edit the VBA code** of a macro. Finally, you learned how to create **custom functions**.

Unit 8

In this unit, you learned how to **publish a workbook as a Web page**. Next, you learned how to change the data in the source workbook and republish the Web page to reflect those changes. Finally, you learned how to **publish a PivotTable as a Web page**.

Unit 9

In this unit, you learned how to **create a Document Workspace**. You also learned how to **publish** and **view lists** on the SharePoint server. You learned how to **synchronize lists** with data on the SharePoint server.

Topic B: Continued learning after class

It is impossible to learn to use any software effectively in a single day. To get the most out of this class, you should begin working with Excel 2003 to perform real tasks as soon as possible. We also offer resources for continued learning.

Next courses in this series

This is the third course in this series. The next courses in this series are:

- *Excel 2003: Power User*
- *Excel 2003: VBA Programming*

Other resources

For more information, visit www.axzopress.com.

Excel 2003: Advanced

Quick reference

Button	Shortcut keys	Function
		Collapses a dialog box.
		Expands a dialog box.
		Hides details in a PivotTable.
		Shows details in a PivotTable.
		Updates a PivotTable with the latest data.
	ALT + L	Opens the PivotTable Field dialog box.
		Opens the AutoFormat dialog box.
		Copies the contents of a cell.
		Pastes the copied contents into a cell.
		Sets the macro recorder to record relative cell references.
		Stops recording a macro.
		Draws a button on a worksheet.
		Displays the PivotTable Field List window.

Glossary

3-D Name
Refers to the same cell or a range of cells across multiple worksheets.

Arguments
The values that a function uses for calculations.

Comments
Non-executable lines of code used to describe a macro.

Database
A collection of related information.

Data Form
A dialog box that gives you an edit field for each column that doesn't contain a formula.

Data Table
A range that displays the results of changing certain values in one or more formulas.

Document Library
A folder that stores the shared files for a document workspace.

Document Workspace
A Web site based on Microsoft Windows SharePoint Services, that helps you share documents with project team members.

Field
A column of data in a database. Also used to refer to a category of data in a PivotTable.

Function Procedure
Contains the code which, when executed, performs a sequence of steps and then returns a value.

Goal Seek Utility
Used to solve a formula based on the value that you want the formula to return.

HLOOKUP
A horizontal lookup used to find values in a table that has column labels.

Input Cell
The location where various values are substituted from a data table.

Interactivity
A feature that can be added to an Excel worksheet that has been published on the Web, allowing users to work with the published data.

Links List
Displays the links available in a Document Workspace.

Macro
A series of instructions that execute automatically with a single command.

Members List
Displays the names of document-workspace members and their online status.

Microsoft Query
A feature that helps you retrieve data that meets certain conditions in one or more tables of a database.

Module
The special sheets in which VBA code is stored.

Name
A meaningful description that you assign to a cell or range of cells.

Nested Function
Uses a function as an argument of another function.

PivotTable
An interactive table that summarizes, organizes, and compares large amounts of data in a worksheet.

Record
A row of data in a database.

Return Value
The result of a Function procedure.

Scenario
A set of input values that produce different results.

Solver Utility
Performs complex what-if analysis by adjusting the values in multiple cells used in a formula.

Source Data
The data on which a PivotTable is based.

Sub-Procedure
Contains the code which, when executed, performs a sequence of steps.

Tasks List
Helps you assign jobs to other document-workspace members or make a to-do list for yourself.

VBA (Visual Basic for Applications)

The code, or language, in which Excel saves the steps of a macro.

Views

Different sets of worksheet display and print settings that you can save.

VLOOKUP

A vertical lookup used to find values in a table that has row labels.

What-If Analysis

Changing the values in a worksheet and observing how these changes affect the results of the formulas.

XML (Extensible Markup Language)

A set of rules for structuring and designing data formats that are exchanged between applications.

Index